gold

gold

FASHION JEWELRY

Catwalk and Couture

Maia Adams

Laurence King Publishing

LAURENCE KING

First published in 2010
This mini edition published in 2012
by Laurence King Publishing Ltd
361–373 City Road
London EC1V 1LR
United Kingdom
Tel + 44 20 7841 6900
Fax + 44 20 7841 6910
e-mail enquiries@laurenceking.com
www.laurenceking.com

A catalogue record for this book is available
from the British Library

ISBN 978-1-78067-020-1

Cover Design: Masumi Briozzo
Design: & SMITH
Typeface: Berthold Akzidenz Grotesk
Senior Editor: Sophie Page
Printed in China

Half title: Pencil and gouache sketches from Philip Crangi's Notebook
Frontispiece: 'Run Over Floral Neckpiece' from Michelle Jank's Airs and Social Disgraces' collection AW08

Contents

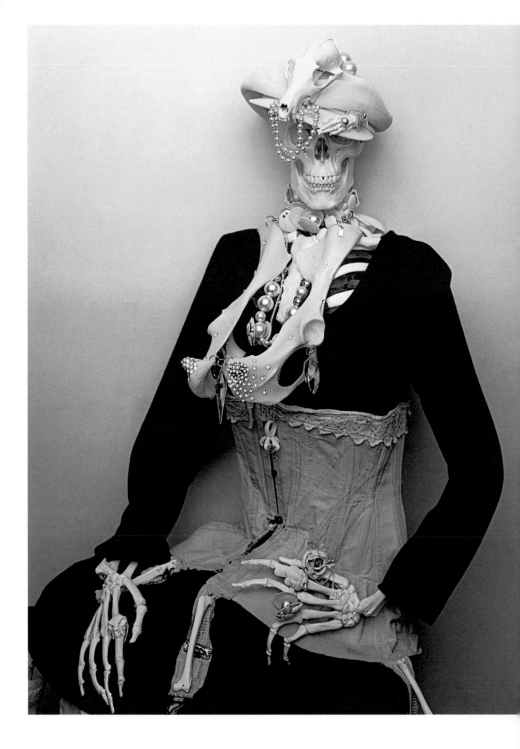

Introduction

'Why do we wear jewellery? Because we crave attention and decorating ourselves is a great way to get it. When you break it down, that's it, we just want to be noticed.' Alexis Bittar

It is perhaps no coincidence that in financially-straightened times jewellery, with its glamorous connotations and endless scope for enhancing individual style, has been heralded as the perfect way to rejuvenate our wardrobes without breaking the bank. From high street to high end, at no other time has it enjoyed such prominence, but it is within the field of contemporary designer fashion that the form is undergoing its most remarkable transformation. After seasons of it-bags and to-die-for shoes, designer fashion jewellery has captured our imaginations, exploding into a new language of adornment as a vibrant array of jewels drip from magazine pages, dominate style barometers and fuel debates on the outfit-enlivening merits of the right bit of bling.

Economic factors may have played a part in jewellery's renaissance, but the breadth and originality filtering through is down to the unfettered vision of a growing number of independent jewellery-makers who are pushing the boundaries of their creativity and the expectations of their peers by rewriting the rules. Among their ranks are those whose fine jewellery sensibilities and training see them apply classic methods to contemporary jewellery-making, and those whose background in art jewellery casts a conceptual slant on their work. That many of them work simultaneously as stylists, photographers and fashion, costume or product designers means that they bring an eclectic arsenal of techniques and influences to bear on a body of work that runs the gamut from craft-based to technology-led; cerebral to silly; witty to whimsical. Whatever the project, their work represents the spirit of couture for the twenty-first century, showcasing skilled craftsmanship, unusual materials and an often limited-edition approach. As jeweller Scott Stephen puts it, 'Designer fashion jewellery by its nature packs more of a punch. Size, shape, form – anything's possible.'

What unites this otherwise disparate group is the impact they are having on the fashion industry as a result of collaborations with fashion designers, the production of their own bi-annual 'fashion' jewellery lines and the appearance of their work in editorial and catwalk shows.

As designer fashion jewellery becomes a viable way of expanding the brand message – and what was previously a niche market has become big business – luxury fashion labels without dedicated in-house design teams are drafting in independent jewellery makers as long-term consultants or to create capsule collections and catwalk showpieces of the kind demonstrated in this book. Such ventures are symbiotic: jewellery makers enjoy a raised profile or the financial wherewithal to use materials (and learn skills) otherwise unavailable to them; the brands gain kudos by association with jewellers who are design stars in their own right, or with an edgy young name.

In an industry that feeds on the thrill of the new this dynamic medium offers scope for eternal reinvention and with designer fashion jewellery evolving at an unprecedented pace, jewellery makers are looking for ways to extend their visual vocabulary. According to Valery Demure, a London-based agent who has brokered collaborations between some of the world's top fashion jewellers and brands such as Comme des Garçons and Repetto, 'What is important is to encourage designers to develop their jewellery skills into things such as accessory design,

garment embellishment and footwear. It's in this cross-pollination of ideas that exciting things happen.'

It would be disingenuous to suggest that this is the first time that jewellery has enjoyed a moment in the fashion spotlight. As one of the oldest forms of body adornment – used to denote status, celebrate rites of passage and enhance our beauty – it has formed an essential part of our sartorial repertoire since time immemorial. It was not until the twentieth century, however, that fashion jewellery came into its own. During the 20s Coco Chanel's pioneering use of costume jewellery challenged the status quo that jewels were only for the very wealthy. By the 60s Paco Rabanne was designing futuristic jewellery with wood, plastic and paper to complement his 'space-age' fashions and Kenneth Jay Lane was creating fabulous fakes for Jackie Onassis and Elizabeth Taylor. The 80s were dominated by Butler & Wilson with their supersized imitation jewels, and Madonna baited the mainstream in rubber bangles and crucifixes designed by New York scenester, Maripol. As the century drew to a close jewellery's re-emergence onto the catwalks of designers such as Thierry Mugler and Hussein Chalayan

marked the end of a lengthy reign of minimalism and the start of a more experimental approach to fashion jewellery. Initiatives such as Swarovski Runway Rocks in 2005 and Coutts London Jewellery week in 2008 demonstrated that it had become a discipline in its own right. The Jewels for Fashion symposium held at Geneva's University of Art and Design indicated a desire for intellectual inquiry about the burgeoning impact of jewellery on fashion.

What distinguishes contemporary fashion jewellery from its costume predecessors is the ethos that underscores it. As Erickson Beamon's Vicki Beamon says, 'Costume is an antiquated term for jewellery that, on the whole, was designed to look real.' This new breed of designer fashion jewellery makes no such claims – its purpose is not to imitate but to innovate.

Recently, fashion's love of statement necklaces blossomed into an affair with lobe-taxing earrings and supersized bangles but where other fashion fads dart from oh-so-now to so-last-season in the blink of an eye jewellery, with its ability to be simultaneously frivolous and symbolically potent, has an enduring appeal that will keep it top of our wishlists for some time to come.

PREVIOUS PAGE A SELECTION OF JEWELLERY FROM YOSHIKO CREATION'S 'LE FOSSILE' COLLECTION SS07 **ABOVE RIGHT** 'BUBBLE' NECKLACE FLORIAN 2004 **OPPOSITE, LEFT** MODEL WEARING JEWELLERY FROM 'BLESS NO12 TEAM-UPS – THE JEWELLERY' **OPPOSITE, RIGHT** A PAGE FROM THE LOOKBOOK THAT ACCOMPANIED SABRINA DEHOFF'S 'LITTLE HELPERS' COLLECTION AW08

'Jewellery is such a wonderful way to celebrate being human – this strange mess of mind and body, imagination and matter.'

FLORIAN LADSTÄTTER

Alexis Bittar

IF EVER A TALE EPITOMIZED THE AMERICAN DREAM, ALEXIS BITTAR'S LIFE STORY IS IT. SPECIALIZING IN HAND-CARVED, COLOUR-CENTRIC LUCITE JEWELLERY, BITTAR WENT FROM HAWKING HIS WARES ON THE STREETS OF NEW YORK CITY TO PRESIDING OVER A GLOBAL BUSINESS EMPIRE. AND THAT, HE SAYS, IS JUST FOR STARTERS.

'If it wasn't for the excitement that I get from fashion I'd be bored shitless,' avows Alexis Bittar. 'What drew me to jewellery in the first place was actually my love of fashion. I get a thrill out of creating jewellery that fits into an era so that in the future people can look back and gauge what was happening back in the day.'

In 1982, aged just thirteen, Bittar started selling vintage jewellery and clothes on the streets of New York's East Village. 'MTV was starting out so you could still find really underground movements whose fashions were incredibly inspiring,' he says of the scene at the time. After a period selling 1930s Bakelite jewellery he realized that people bought it because they were drawn to the fact it was hand-carved. Looking around at the 80s' penchant for mass-produced, moulded plastic jewellery Bittar had a brainwave. 'I bought a block of Lucite and started hand-carving it as if it was a precious material. A year later I dropped out of college to sell the Lucite pieces on the street full time. After that, selling to stores was easy.'

As Bittar's empire grew stylists such as *Vogue*'s Grace Coddington and Patti Wilson began to take note, asking him to produce bespoke pieces for their shoots. Bittar says that to this day he still gets excited at seeing his work on the pages of *Vogue* or *iD*: 'I look forward to seeing my fantasy become a reality on the glossy pages.' Asked to pinpoint a moment when he knew he'd become a success Bittar tells of the time stylist Laurie Goldstein commissioned a piece for an Estée Lauder campaign starring Carolyn Murphy. 'It's amazing the impact one good stylist using your work can have on your reputation. That image, with my glowing jewellery, went worldwide and suddenly everyone

understood how alluring Lucite could be.' Although today the staff in his New York studio number in excess of 160, Bittar still personally hand carves the prototype of every new design for each of his three collections: Lucite, Elements and Miss Havisham. And the measure of affection he feels for his work is indicated by the fact that he ascribes female personas to his collections: Elements, with its feminine and eclectic mix of precious and semi-precious rough-cut stones and hammered metal, is 'a pot-head girlie from Santa Barbara smoking a joint', while Miss Havisham, the newest member of the trio, started out with 'a totally schizophrenic personality' but has calmed down somewhat to become 'what Grace Jones would wear in the 80s'. In translation this equates to sculpted metal cuffs and necklaces that reference Brancusi's large metal sculptures and knotted cord chokers festooned with gold discs, pearls and ice-like Lucite slivers. Of his frequent and

affectionate references to the 80s Bittar says simply: 'I can't stop flying the flag for that decade. It had such an impact on me so it sneaks into every collection.'

But it's Bittar's signature line, Lucite, that has become his leading lady. Each piece is made from blocks of acrylic that are whittled down into chunky cuffs, elaborate earrings and fanciful cocktail rings. Colours and patterns are then hand painted, and embellishments such as crystals, studs or gilding are manually applied. Despite the couture nature of his work – every piece is hand sculpted and painted – Bittar claims that fashion's ready-to-wear model is what informs his outlook. 'Anyone can crank out crap but I prove that you can sell to 600 stores worldwide and create jewellery that is thought-provoking. Not in a life-changing way but just to make people stop and look and say 'Wow, I've never seen that before.'

The stop-and-stare nature of his work has led to a handful of high-profile fashion

collaborations over the years. In 1999 he designed Burberry's first couture jewellery collection, painting the brand's iconic plaid onto bold Lucite pieces. For Michael Kors' ss08 catwalk collection he created coloured resin pieces and metal shapes that were 'late 60s: Barbarella meets Woody Allen's Sleeper' and in the same season his muse for Tuleh's show was 'an Italian woman during the 60s in an amazing coral necklace'.

Asked where he gets his drive from, Bittar says it's borne of a desire to keep creating: 'I work all the time and I think incredibly quickly, so much so that when I'm explaining to my assistants I have to try not to talk in tongues. We do three collections twice a year so I don't really have time to do an amazing watercolour for each piece. And anyway, I'm so A.D.D that I move on straight away. When it comes to the possibility of creating something new and pushing the envelope I'm like a little kid.'

WWW.ALEXISBITTAR.COM

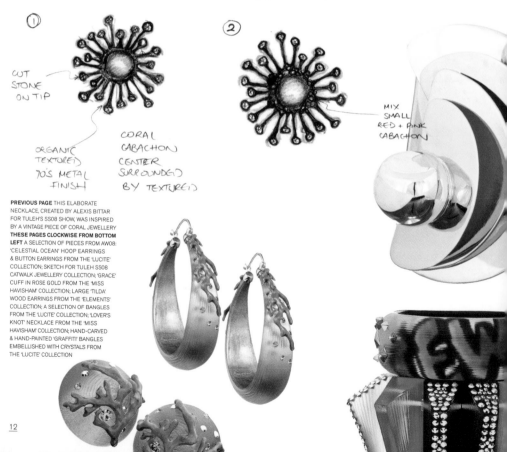

CUT STONE ON TIP

ORGANIC TEXTURED 70'S METAL FINISH

CORAL CABACHON CENTER SURROUNDED BY TEXTURED

MIX SMALL RED + PINK CABACHON

PREVIOUS PAGE THIS ELABORATE NECKLACE, CREATED BY ALEXIS BITTAR FOR TULEH'S SS08 SHOW, WAS INSPIRED BY A VINTAGE PIECE OF CORAL JEWELLERY **THESE PAGES CLOCKWISE FROM BOTTOM LEFT** A SELECTION OF PIECES FROM AW08: 'CELESTIAL OCEAN' HOOP EARRINGS & BUTTON EARRINGS FROM THE 'LUCITE' COLLECTION; SKETCH FOR TULEH SS08 CATWALK JEWELLERY COLLECTION; 'GRACE' CUFF IN ROSE GOLD FROM THE 'MISS HAVISHAM' COLLECTION; LARGE 'TILDA' WOOD EARRINGS FROM THE 'ELEMENTS' COLLECTION; A SELECTION OF BANGLES FROM THE 'LUCITE' COLLECTION; 'LOVER'S KNOT' NECKLACE FROM THE 'MISS HAVISHAM' COLLECTION; HAND-CARVED & HAND-PAINTED 'GRAFFITI' BANGLES EMBELLISHED WITH CRYSTALS FROM THE 'LUCITE' COLLECTION

'That image, with my glowing jewellery, went worldwide and suddenly everyone understood how alluring Lucite could be.'

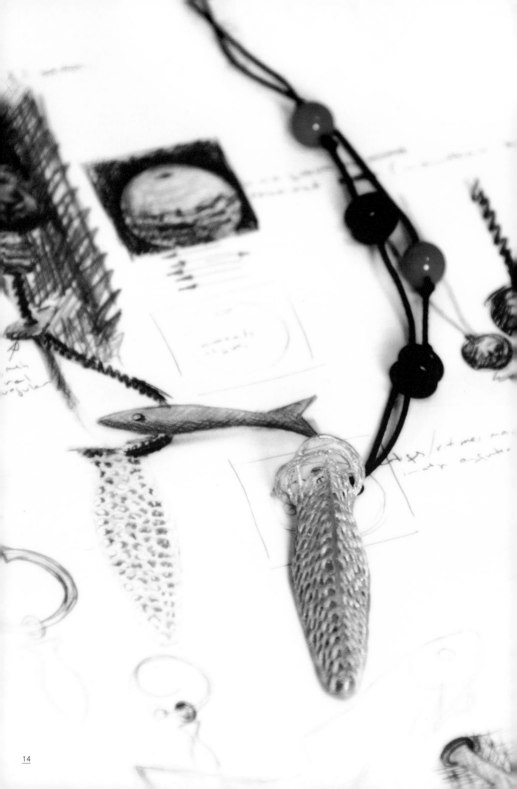

Annabcn

BARCELONA-BASED JEWELLERY BRAND ANNABCN HAS ONE MOTTO: TO KEEP THINGS SIMPLE. 'WE LET OURSELVES BE SEDUCED BY EVERYDAY THINGS: LIGHT, COLOUR, TEXTURES, SMELLS, THE PEOPLE WE MEET AND WHATEVER MAKES US SMILE,' EXPLAINS FOUNDER ANNA GONZÁLEZ. 'THOSE ARE THE LITTLE THINGS WE TRANSLATE INTO OUR JEWELLERY.'

Anna González came to jewellery design late in life. Born into a large family of scientists the artistically-inclined González forged an early career in PR until, at the age of forty-three, the desire for a more creative outlet led her to enroll on a course to study visual arts and jewellery design. While at the college she met Maria Josep Forcadell who, in quick succession, went from being González's design tutor to close friend to business partner and collaborator.

In 2005 González set up her jewellery design company Annabcn Spielt und Baut. The name – abbreviated for commercial purposes to Annabcn – is a fusion of Catalan and German (González is fluent in both) that summarizes the company philosophy. As a universally recognized name, Anna represents feminine spirit and the multi-cultural background of its founder. BCN is an abbreviation of Barcelona – the town where the company was founded and where the Annabcn boutique is located. Spielt und Baut, German for play and build, alludes to the way González and Forcadell experiment with form and materials.

González and Forcadell enjoy a relaxed attitude to work; an approach, González suggests, that may have something to do with their enviable lifestyles. Their proximity to the beach and the year-round balmy climate of their Mediterranean home informs their temperaments. Moreover, in keeping with their pared-down approach each of Annabcn's own-line collections (both men's and women's) is inspired from one season to the next by a running theme – the natural environment. As collection names such as Gifts from the Sea, Jewels from the Earth, and Fruits from the Garden suggest, Mother Nature is the muse who inspires themes or directions in which found objects, colour and texture play a key role.

'We never pick things for their monetary value or how easy they are to use,' says González of their eclectic materials. 'It's about what they can bring to the final piece.'

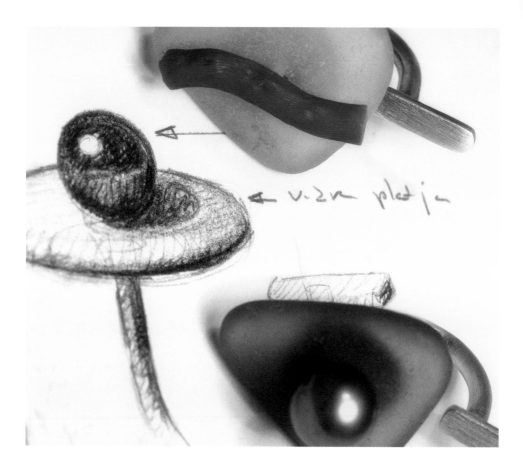

Tahitian pearls – something of a signature – are frequently paired with fabrics such as suede, silk, felt and tulle. Snail shells, driftwood, PVC, enamel and Mediterranean coral are incongruously presented together, either in their natural state or cast in gold and silver. The diverse result ensures that, despite recurring themes, the work itself is far from repetitive: while some pieces are craft-like in sensibility others – such as pearls bound into neoprene rings – have a more directional aesthetic. 'The challenge is to remain creative and reinvent oneself collection after collection or piece after piece,' says González. 'We don't like typecasting because ultimately it usurps creative freedom.'

In 2008 Annabcn were invited by Paris-based fashion designer Boris Bidjan Saberi to design a 20-piece jewellery collection for his ss09 menswear catwalk show. Once again, their quest for simplicity was a driving factor and for inspiration González looked to a group of children for whom she runs arts courses in her spare time: 'They taught me that something uncomplicated, even primitive and rough, can be elegant so that became my jumping-off point.'

The resulting collection was based on found objects including pieces of iron, nails, branches and seeds. These were rendered in solid silver and combined with offcuts from the linens, furs and cottons from which the garments were constructed to create a range of rings, necklaces, pendants, bracelets and key rings. In addition, using ultra-fine chains to create a transparent effect with metal, González and Forcadell produced a necklace and a burka designed to reflect the designer's Persian roots.

Of Annabcn's debut onto the international fashion circuit González admits that she found the experience thrilling: 'That was a completely new world for us. It taught us to become more open and at the same time to understand that not every idea is valid; that the editing process is probably the hardest and most important lesson a designer has to learn.' And on the matter of designing jewellery specifically for a fashion market González is unequivocal: 'We believe that our jewellery belongs firmly in the twenty-first century and since art and fashion are reflections of the moment in history in which they appear we take it as a given that our work has to be suitable for the way people dress in the time in which we live. That, to us, is the essence of fashion. Style, on the other hand, comes from within.'

WWW.ANNABCN.COM

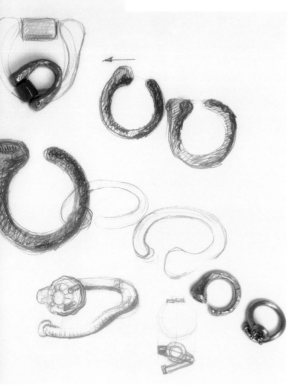

INSPIRED BY NATURE AND NATURAL
FORMS ANNABCN CREATE JEWELLERY
USING FOUND OBJECTS SUCH AS PIECES
OF CORAL AND SEA-SMOOTHED PIECES
OF GLASS. **PREVIOUS PAGE** 'MERMAID
CONTAINER' 2006 **OPPOSITE** 'FRUITS
OF THE OCEAN' 2005 **THIS PAGE,
CLOCKWISE FROM LEFT** 'FRUITS OF
THE MINE' 2005; NAIL RINGS FOR BORIS
BIDJAN SABERI'S SS09 CATWALK SHOW;
NAIL PENDANT FOR BORIS BIDJAN
SABERI'S SS09 CATWALK SHOW

OPPOSITE MODEL WEARING A VEIL
MADE FROM SILVER CHAINS DESIGNED
BY ANNABCN FOR BORIS BIDJAN SABERI'S
SS09 CATWALK SHOW **ABOVE** PINE-LEAF
PENDANTS DESIGNED BY ANNABCN FOR
BORIS BIDJAN SABERI'S SS09
CATWALK SHOW

'Since art and
fashion are reflections
of the moment in
history in which
they appear, we take
it as a given that
our work has to
be suitable for the
way people dress
in the time in which
we live. That, to us,
is the essence of
fashion. Style, on the
other hand, comes
from within.'

Arielle
De Pinto

PREVIOUS PAGES MASK 2008 & FLAT
MASK 2009. RIGHT FRINGE POUCH 2009
OPPOSITE LATTICE COLLAR 2009; CLASSIC
RIBBON NECKLACE 2009; SKETCH FOR
TRIANGLE FLAG NECKLACE 2008

CANADIAN DESIGNER ARIELLE DE PINTO'S IDIOSYNCRATIC APPROACH TO MAKING JEWELLERY DEVELOPED IN DIRECT RESPONSE TO HER ITINERANT LIFESTYLE. BUT WHILE CREATING HER UNIQUE BRAND OF HAND-CROCHETED METAL JEWELLERY MAY DEMAND FEW TOOLS, STRONG FINGERS, A CAN-DO ATTITUDE AND EXTREME PATIENCE ARE A MUST.

Arielle de Pinto is the first to admit she finds the jewellery-making process deeply unpleasant: 'The physical act of crocheting chain is so disagreeable that I find myself engaged in a perpetual battle with the material.' But in a manner that suggests an every-cloud-has-a-silver-lining approach to life de Pinto is quick to look on the bright side. 'I like to work with no preconceptions about the outcome and crocheting has really taught me patience and how to channel a flow. I believe in a kind of energy that one puts forward, and I find the more I worry about the tiny details the more that energy gets disrupted.'

It was at college in Montreal that de Pinto developed a talent for crocheting silver and vermeil chains. Throwing a contemporary

spin on a traditional craft she began creating web-like jewellery and masks that were simultaneously delicate, tactile, weighty and – in the case of the masks – some might argue, a touch disturbing.

The impetus to turn her hobby into a living came during a print internship in New York where cleaning sinks and toilets left de Pinto feeling, perhaps not surprisingly, unfulfilled. She showed a couple of crocheted pieces to American designer Judi Rosen who immediately put them on sale in her boutique The Good, The Bad And The Ugly. Sales to other Manhattan stores and a mention in The New York Times' style section followed and de Pinto spent the rest of her school year crocheting in class to keep up with demand.

After graduating in 2007 de Pinto decided to make a road trip from Montreal to New York where she planned to set up home on arrival. On her first day on the road she received a call informing her that she had been nominated for an accessory design award. The news spurred de Pinto into action: 'On the road I established a collection, put together a look book, and scouted boutiques in every city we passed through. A month later I arrived in New York for fashion week and met up with all the buyers I'd encountered on the trip.'

A similar charm offensive at other fashion events, including Parisian trade show Rendez-Vous and Berlin's Ideal, won de Pinto more accounts – and a lot more time on the road. 'I didn't have an apartment for

'I want wearing my jewellery to be something one barely has to think about. I don't want people to obsess over it and I don't want my work to be treated like something too precious.'

PENNANT FLAG

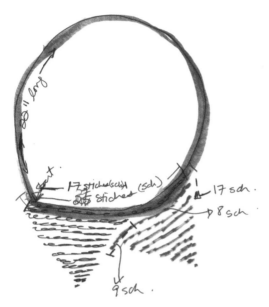

30" long

17 stiches(sch) (sch)
stiched
17 sch.
8 sch.
9 sch.

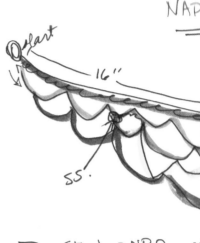

NAP

start
16"

SS.

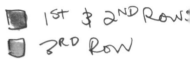
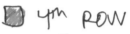

1ST & 2ND ROWS
3RD ROW
4TH ROW
5TH ROW
6TH ROW

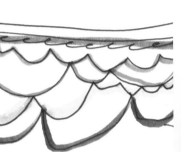

about a year but I did hone my technique so that I could be completely mobile. It's remarkable how much work I got done in cafés, parks, airplanes, public places. All I needed was chain, some oxidizer and a few hooks.'

Elaborating on her working methods de Pinto points to a printmaking elective that taught her a valuable lesson: 'My approach is really messy but it's a controlled mess. That's the most valuable thing printmaking taught me because it's a medium that provides for a lot of experimentation but also demands precision. If you get one fingerprint on something it will be there on the next hundred things you produce. Consequently, I love to work with rigid

techniques in which I give the material just the right amount of freedom without letting it overrule my intention.'

Her aim is to make pieces that are very easy to wear – hence the apparently unrefined approach she adopts to finishing each piece which entails leaving a few chain threads to hang loose and rarely even using clasps. 'I want wearing my jewellery to be something one barely has to think about. I don't want people to obsess over it and I don't want my work to be treated like something too precious: it tarnishes, the oxidization fades, and with wear the pieces loosen and adjust to their owners.' Having said that, she adds as a caveat: 'I wouldn't want the appreciable amount of work and

attention to detail to be disregarded. It's obvious that each piece is made by hand, and is something completely personal.'

With international distribution sorted, and a clear design direction established, de Pinto is eager to conquer new projects. The key, she says, is to take time out: 'When I get too busy with production and the business aspects of things, I get scared that I am not spending enough time just hanging out and working at a leisurely pace. It's ridiculous how much – apparently – dead time I need to conceptualize and push out new work. Now, to grow creatively, I need the freedom to experiment in a studio and have a less transitory existence.'

WWW.ARIELLEDEPINTO.COM

Atelier 11

ATELIER 11'S MISSION STATEMENT IS SIMPLE: 'WE WANT TO CHANGE PEOPLE'S RUSTED IDEAS ABOUT JEWELLERY, WHAT IT STANDS FOR AND WHAT IT SHOULD LOOK LIKE.' WITH TONGUE-IN-CHEEK HUMOUR AS THEIR WEAPON OF CHOICE THEY HAVE BUILT A BRAND OF HIS-AND-HERS JEWELLERY THAT AIMS TO FLIP ANTIQUATED NOTIONS OF THE FORM FIRMLY ON THEIR HEAD.

In 1999 Antwerp-based Flor Janssens, Ludovik Colpaert and Elke L. Peeters set up Atelier 11 – a design studio geared towards challenging received notions of what jewellery should be. 'Too many people still think of jewellery in terms of gold, silver, pearls and diamonds,' claims Colpaert. 'We try to show them that contemporary jewellery can also be fun and what's more, that it's entirely possible to be experimental and still be commercial.'

Having studied jewellery design at Antwerp's Sint Lucas Antwerpen college Janssens and Colpaert (Peeters left the business in 2006) apply art jewellery techniques to products aimed at a fashion audience. 'Art jewellery is complicated, conceptual and expensive and the designs only reach the few people who visit galleries,' Janssens explains. 'We want to use our skills to reach more people with our collections and to make great jewellery that is affordable for each wallet.'

Having established a successful women's line, in December 2003 they opened their first flagship store in Antwerp and two years later they launched a men's line which, in a sense, is the embodiment of their toned-down ethos. On the challenges of designing jewellery for men Colpaert says: 'Men don't shop like women. A woman, for example, will wear green earrings just because they match with her dress. Men, however, don't wear jewellery simply for decoration but to express themselves, which means that when they buy they're looking for a very particular design.' Consequently Atelier 11's sterling silver trinkets tend to be direct, no nonsense and sport little extraneous decoration other than the occasional photoprint and colour applied by powdercoating – a painting technique used for cars – which has become an Atelier 11 trademark.

The themes around which they base both men's and women's collections often allude humorously to classic gender-specific interests and dreams: Hollywood divas, Atlantis and fairytales for her; space travel, superheroes and polar expeditions for him. A classic embodiment of this approach was X-plore – their men's ss07 collection that challenged notions of travel in today's digital times by asking whether facts, figures and pictures on a screen replace the perception of our senses. The resulting jewellery included silver charm necklaces sporting tiny spanners, mini-torches and tiger pendants, USB and jack-plug pendants and bungee cord bracelets: an arsenal of amulets for contemporary armchair explorers.

Colpaert and Janssens believe that the Belgian inclination towards modesty influences their approach to work. 'We are very discreet people. We don't like glamour or being in the spotlight so it's our designs that count,' explains Colpaert. He is adamant, however, that simplicity should not be confused with lack of thought. 'When you look at our work you will see that our collections are far from easy. We put a lot of humour into our collections and we're not afraid to experiment with uncommon materials and shapes. Nevertheless, we strongly believe that a concept should never be so complicated that it needs explanation, and we don't see the point in making experiments that no soul would wear. Therefore we use popular themes and recognizable images to make our point.'

In 2001 Atelier 11 were appointed as artistic manufacturers of Raf Simons' jewellery. In this role they are responsible for providing assistance and technical design solutions, as well as organizing selling, production and distribution of Simons' jewellery. Building on this high-profile association Colpaert and Janssens have gone on to collaborate with a wide range of avant-garde fashion designers including Martin Margiela, Veronique Branquinho, Anne Demeulemeester, Viktor & Rolf and AF Vandevorst. Each project has presented its own inherent challenges but has also taught them new skills and ways of tackling a brief. 'Every designer has a totally unique world he or she lives in so the way their ideas take form are always different to our own collections,' explains Janssens. 'Fashion designers often don't understand the technical limitations of what we do so they come to us with ideas that are technically impossible.' Bearing these demands in mind, Janssens believes his task as a jewellery expert is to breathe life into those ideas while simultaneously adding to his own skills base. 'In this way we cross borders. We look for solutions that are not meant for jewellery. We look for crazy ways to make crazy things.'

When asked if, in the grand scheme of things, jewellery is important Colpaert is philosophical: 'You can ask the same question about art. Although it's not really necessary for us to survive, it has been around since men made fire so it must be important to us.' Janssens, displaying the phlegmatic Belgian character to a tee, answers simply but firmly, 'Of course!'

WWW.ATELIERELF.COM

'We look for solutions that are not meant for jewellery. We look for crazy ways to make crazy things.'

PREVIOUS PAGE A MODEL BACKSTAGE AT THE AF VANDEVORST SS09 CATWALK SHOW
WEARS A NECKLACE DESIGNED BY ATELIER 11. **LEFT AND ABOVE LEFT** JEWELLERY
DESIGNED BY ATELIER 11 FOR RAF SIMONS SS04 **ABOVE** JEWELLERY DESIGNED
BY ATELIER 11 FOR AF VANDEVORST AW07

OPPOSITE RING BRACELET DESIGNED BY ATELIER 11 FOR MAISON MARTIN MARGIELA'S 'COLLECTION ARTISANAL' AW04 **THIS PAGE, CLOCKWISE FROM BOTTOM LEFT** 'DUCK AND GUN' NECKLACE FROM THE 'OPPOSITES ATTRACT' MEN'S COLLECTION SS04; PIECES FROM THE 'SOME LIKE IT HOT' WOMEN'S COLLECTION AW08; 'TWO GUNS' FROM THE 'BOYS WILL BE BOYS' COLLECTION AW05; RING DESIGNED BY ATELIER 11 FOR MAISON MARTIN MARGIELA'S 'COLLECTION ARTISANAL' AW04

'We try to show that contemporary jewellery can also be fun and what's more, that it's entirely possible to be experimental and still remain commercial.'

Bless

INCONGRUOUSLY NAMED AFTER A BERLIN BAKERY, BLESS IS A DESIGN STUDIO FOUNDED IN 1997 BY GERMAN-BORN INES KAAG AND AUSTRIAN, DESIREE HEISS. IN JUXTAPOSING UNORTHODOX ELEMENTS AND CHALLENGING EXPECTATIONS, BLESS' WORK SUBVERTS NORMS AND FORCES THE VIEWER TO DOUBLE-TAKE. TO BLESS, THE JEWELLERY THEY CREATE IS JUST ANOTHER MEANS OF PROVOKING THOUGHT BY QUESTIONING THE STATUS QUO.

Bless are difficult to pigeonhole and they like it that way. Exploring a different means of expression each season Bless projects – be they products, exhibitions or collaborations – range from highly functional forms to propositions so conceptual they verge on abstraction. Spanning the fields of art, design, architecture and fashion, Bless escape easy definition by creating products and distribution systems that do not fit into any pre-established category. Each project is simply given a number and an idiosyncratic name that is often a made-up word.

Adopting an ambiguous stance Heiss and Kaag say they see fashion as a subjective space that is adaptable, multifunctional and open to infinite possibilities. 'We are more interested in creating "new classics" which is why we often make accessories which are more or less decorative,' explains Heiss. 'The jewellery pieces we design are simply Bless products and equivalent to a pair of shoes or other accessories.' They do, however, allow that the advantage of constructing jewellery from inexpensive materials means 'it does not necessarily have to be "in fashion" for ages, so it can be more exaggerated, more special and more interesting.'

Their leftfield approach has won them a legion of design-savvy fans as well as collaborations with companies keen to acquire the sheen of intellectual credibility that Bless bring to their projects. When Swiss jewellery brand Bucherer invited them to collaborate on a project Kaag and Heiss decided to explore notions of inheritance and the effect the passage of time has on an object's sentimental and monetary value. As a starting point they posed a series of questions: What does it mean to buy jewellery? How does jewellery become increasingly loaded with energy and personality as it changes owners? How does the context in which jewellery is displayed affect its emotional charge? Using discarded gold and silver chains and old charms they created the

PREVIOUS PAGE MODEL WEARING JEWELLERY FROM 'BLESS Nº12 TEAM-UPS – THE JEWELLERY' **OPPOSITE, BELOW LEFT** 'FRONTSPOILER' FROM 'BLESS Nº23 – THE BRINGER' **OPPOSITE, TOP LEFT** A DISPLAY OF BLESS JEWELLERY IN ONE OF BLESS' POP-UP SHOPS BACKGROUND SELECTED DESIGNS FROM 'BLESS Nº12 TEAM-UPS – THE JEWELLERY', **LEFT** 'BLESS Nº12 TEAM-UPS – THE JEWELLERY' **BELOW** 'BLESS Nº18 ALLROUNDWEAR' BUTTON SET

'We are more interested in creating "new classics" which is why we often make accessories which are more or less decorative.'

Materialmix collection – a series of necklaces and bracelets that were later incorporated in the project Bless N°12 Team-Ups: Co Produced Visions of Personal Landscapes.

Other jewellery-inspired projects followed. For Berlin's Designmai showcase in 2005 Bless N°26 Cable Jewellery once again explored notions of re-contextualizing pre-existing components, this time with a more aesthetically challenging outcome: Indian bangles, rhinestones, bamboo, dyed black rosewood and pearls intertwined with USB ports and phone cables.

Two projects later Bless N°28 Climate Confusion Assistance saw Kaag and Heiss create a series of Ring Gloves – knitted fingers with gold rings attached – and Bless N°31 Ohyescoolgreat featured dual-purpose Winter Necklaces – knitted wool and mohair necklettes hung with gold-plated or silver chains. Most recently Bless N°36 – Nothingneath boasted Fringe Glasses whose lenses were obscured by nickel chain curtains. Pressed for an explanation Kaag would say only, 'There was no specific thinking behind it – everybody is very welcome to think whatever.'

Kaag and Heiss met as students at a design competition in Paris. Of their subsequent relationship Kaag says, 'From the moment we met we realized that what we have is very precious and rare.' Indeed their attuned level of mutual understanding means that even geography – Kaag works from Berlin while Heiss remains in Paris – is no barrier to their success. When developing an idea there is no specific recipe or formula – each venture grows differently in a manner the duo liken to a staircase of ideas, some projects having only one or two steps, others seemingly never ending. If there is a unifying theme underscoring Bless' achievements it is a distinctive sense of humour that is reflected in their work. 'It's not that we try to be funny but it's true that we do seem to laugh a lot while we're doing it.'

In April 2000, in response to a growing number of invitations to take part in a variety of art and design exhibitions, Bless introduced the concept of a short-lived nomad shop to their portfolio. Dedicated to retrospectives and special projects Bless N°11 Bless Shops was born. To date their pop-up boutiques have appeared in 15 cities worldwide and the first permanent Bless shop was launched in Berlin in 2003 with a Parisian branch opening shortly thereafter. Bless wares, including jewellery, are available for purchase in each shop which – whether pop-up or permanent – is adapted to suit the circumstances of its new environment. In their own words 'Bless does not promote any style – Bless fits every style.'
WWW.BLESS-SERVICE.DE

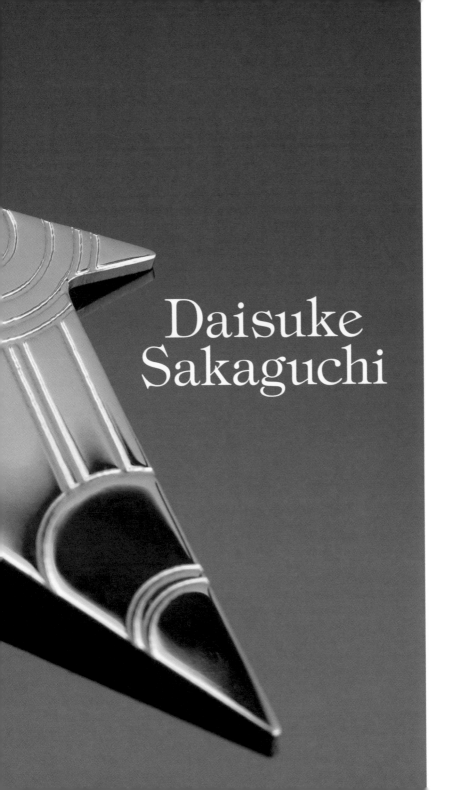

Daisuke
Sakaguchi

DESIGNERS OFTEN CITE STREET CULTURE AS A SOURCE OF INSPIRATION. BUT WHILE THERE ARE THOSE WHO DIP IN AND OUT AS THE NEED FOR CREDIBILITY DICTATES, DAISUKE SAKAGUCHI PRACTICES WHAT HE PREACHES. FROM HIS GRAFFITI WALL MURALS TO HIS GRAF-INFLUENCED JEWELLERY, SAKAGUCHI TRANSLATES HIS SURROUNDINGS INTO HIS ART. AS HE SAYS: 'THE STREETS ARE A PUBLIC CATWALK INVITING YOU TO DISPLAY YOUR WORK AND PROVIDING THE OPPORTUNITY TO SHOW OTHERS YOUR STYLE.'

As the London-born son of Japanese parents Daisuke Sakaguchi's mixed cultural heritage plays an important role in his creativity. 'My work, how I think, how I design all are affected by a combination of Japanese and British culture. It's equal parts sovereign rings and Samurai swords.'

From an early age Sakaguchi was drawn to fashion but using fabrics and designing garments didn't appeal. 'What I like is creating 3D objects. Growing up I loved cartoons like Transformers and one of the things that intrigued me was what the robots and spaceships might look like in real life.' As a teenager Sakaguchi's love of up-tempo, fast

melody music (everything from jazz and Miami bass to garage and grime) and a desire to create artworks that 'looked how the music sounds', were the reason he got into graffiti. 'Putting my passions together made me realise that jewellery was the perfect platform. For me jewellery became loud three-dimensional objects that can be worn on the body as the focal point of an outfit.'

After gaining a BA in jewellery design from Central Saint Martins Sakaguchi launched his first jewellery collection in 2005. An order from Comme des Garçons' Dover Street Market launched him onto fashion's radar and his hip hop-style

knuckledusters, bracelets and necklaces were soon sought-after by influential stylists, including Nicola Formichetti, Patti Wilson and Charlotte Stockdale.

Sakaguchi's street credentials have also seen him work with brands including Adidas, Dr Martens and Nike, for whom he created a bespoke jewellery collection to celebrate the iconic Nike Air Force One sneaker's 25th anniversary. His contribution to the project was 25 unique sterling silver pendants that puzzled together to depict the number 25. Each pendant was acid etched with Sakaguchi's interpretation of the Nike Air Force One's sole print.

'My work, how I think, how I design all are affected by a combination of Japanese and British culture. It's equal parts sovereign rings and Samurai swords.'

But while the streets are his catwalk of choice, Sakaguchi is no stranger to the real thing. In 2006, after designing a men's jewellery collection for ultra-hip Japanese fashion store Oki-Ni, he presented a solo jewellery show at Tokyo Fashion Week. The following September he created pieces for Philip Treacy's aw06 London Fashion Week catwalk show and his bold jewellery aesthetic has latterly been applied to products, including a range of silver dog tags, jacket toggles and mobile phone accessories. More recently, together with avid watch collector Wendy Meakin, he launched WDMS: a series of commission-based fine art pieces that are executed in the form of jewellery.

Despite his love of fashion Sakaguchi claims that trends are not important to him. When explaining the ethos of what he calls his 'future classic' style he says, 'Of course I take into account what has already been done and what's hot right now but my jewellery needs to have longevity not novelty value. I try my best to think about what hasn't been done yet and fuse that with something traditional. I want my work to be as timeless as possible'.

Sakaguchi sets high standards. His signet rings, bracelets and pendants are executed in gold (yellow, white and rose) that is at least 18ct, and silver which is never less than 925 Sterling. Stones are precious and semi-precious and his working methods are meticulous. For higher volume pieces he makes his own masters before sending them to his manufacturers. For bespoke one-off pieces it is imperative that he creates them himself and all initial designs and concept sketches must be hand drawn. 'It's important that the human element of design is still part of the process. How the hand moves has a direct impact on what shapes are created.' Notions of form and finish are gleaned from car wheel arches, buildings, sneakers, chair carvings and the silhouette of buildings. Of the challenges inherent in creating jewellery he says, 'It's a combination of art and maths. Obviously it has to look good but it has to be wearable and comfortable so you need a sense of ergonomics: how it's going to rest on the wrist, lay on the neck, clasp the finger etc; how it will interact with garments.'

Equally rigorous when it comes to promoting his business Sakaguchi bases his approach on established fashion industry success stories. 'I like seeing how fashion designers market their work, from their window displays all the way through to the choice of music for their catwalk show. Yohji Yamamoto is a case in point. He can be really haute couture and exclusive, but he retains those street credentials too. Just look at his Y3 for Adidas range. He reinforced the notion that sportswear is a legitimate fashionwear choice and that, to me, is really inspirational.'
WWW.DAISUKESAKAGUCHI.CO.UK

OPPOSITE KOI CARP BROOCH DRAWING; TOKYO FASHION WEEK 2006 – CLOTHES AND JEWELLERY BY DAISUKE SAKAGUCHI
BELOW SKETCHES FOR SAKAGUCHI'S LIONHEART RING AND KOI CARP BROOCH

David
& Martin

DAVID ANDERSSON AND MARTIN LASSON MET WHILE STUDYING METALLURGY AT KONSTFACK UNIVERSITY IN STOCKHOLM. THEIR GRADUATION PROJECT, A FULLY-FURNISHED ROOM COMPLETE WITH JEWELLERY, LED TO THE LAUNCH OF THEIR JEWELLERY BRAND DAVID & MARTIN, WHICH HAS GONE ON TO WIN ACCOLADES AND AWARDS, INCLUDING THE *ELLE* MAGAZINE OUTSTANDING JEWELLERY DESIGNER GONG IN 2005. ECLECTIC AND INTELLIGENT, THEIR WORK IS INSPIRED BY ART HOUSE FILM, CONTEMPORARY ART AND CHICKENS.

Why did you decide to specialize in jewellery?
David had worked as a goldsmith before we met at art college and although our studies let us explore lots of media, jewellery was what we both loved most. Even back then we saw the gap between bijouterie and fine jewellery and knew it was an area we wanted to explore.

What influence does coming from Sweden have on your work?
We never used to think it had much bearing but as our work has developed we see that it's quite minimalistic, which is a style often associated with Scandinavian design. Our dark and cold winters undoubtedly have some effect on our aesthetics. It comes naturally to us to reduce things and keep the colour scheme simple: gold, silver, white and black.

What are you working on now?
We're experimenting with super-thin silverplate folded in different ways. We want to make something which looks like a mess but which transforms into an organized structure. It feels like a lot of things – fashion, the economy, art, politics – are in transition right now so we're trying to reflect that. We'll see how it works, if it works.

'Make things that are beautiful and other people tend to like them as well.'

How did the collaboration with Karl Lagerfeld come about?

Margareta van den Bosche, who was the design director at Hennes&Mauritz at the time, used a lot of our jewellery. When Karl did his range for H&M he spotted some of our pieces and commissioned us to create a collection of black-plated cuffs and necklaces for the Lagerfeld Gallery ss05 runway show and later for their store in Paris.

What did you create for Acne Jeans?

Acne sponsored us with jeans and to thank them we gave the marketing manager a bracelet. That led to a meeting with their creative director, which resulted in the Bones jewellery collection and a range of T-shirts. The jewellery was literally cast from chicken bones left over from a lunch we had at the office one day.

What did you learn from these collaborations?

It's important to listen to others but in the end trust your own ideas and don't make them too complicated. Make things that are beautiful and other people tend to like them as well.

What materials do you use?

Silver, gold, resin, wood and some textiles.

How should your jewellery to be worn?

Regardless of whether it's diamonds or fake, or whether you pair it with a cocktail dress or jeans and T-shirt, it's how you wear it that makes it 'fashion' or not. It's all about attitude; the simplest silver chain can definitely be fashion in the right context.

How would you summarize your design philosophy?

We try to offer a strong expression and wearability at a price people can afford. Hopefully wearing our jewellery makes people feel more confident.

What inspires you?

Sometimes it's stories, other times it's something we see, taste or feel. We developed the Chicken Feet collection in 2005 after spotting a very pretty girl on a Shanghai subway munching deep-fried chicken feet and simultaneously flicking through French *Vogue*. In 2007 we were asked to make a limited edition men's piece for a department store in Stockholm. Having recently watched Roman Polanski's *The Tenant* we were both struck by a scene where Trelkovsky (the main character) removes a cabinet in his bedroom behind which there's a hole where he finds a human tooth wrapped in cotton. We liked that surreal, scary moment so we made a tooth bracelet. The 2006 collection we call String of Pearls was basically inspired by sex toys.

PREVIOUS PAGE GOLD-PLATED 'FAITH HOPE CHARITY'
NECKLACE 2001 **THESE PAGES, CLOCKWISE FROM
BOTTOM LEFT** BLACK GOLD CIRCLE CUFF DESIGNED
FOR KARL LAGERFELD'S SS05 CATWALK SHOW; SOLID
GOLD BONE BRACELET CREATED FOR ACNE JEANS;
THE SEX TOY-INSPIRED STRING OF PEARLS NECKLACE
2006; GOLD-PLATED NUMBERS CUFF; BONE LEATHER
BRACELET DESIGNED FOR ACNE JEANS

'It's how you wear jewellery that makes it "fashion" or not It's all about attitude.'

You say trends are not important to you – please elaborate.

It is important that we do what we like, so if we want to make jewellery featuring numbers that's what we do, even if everybody else is doing flowers because we try not to follow the crowd. We view each new collection as an evolution of our existing work; a little like work in progress or an inspirational working archive.

How would you like to develop the David & Martin brand?

We'd like to refine our processes, develop our online shop and take on more collaborations. We also plan to hire more people to make the jewellery so that we can focus on our creative concepts.

How do you keep your work fresh?

Never let ourselves get bored, stay curious, carry on looking for new projects and always keep our minds open.

And how do you relax?

Martin: Hunting, riding my motorbike, diving.
David: Spending time in the forest, sauna, sex.
WWW.DAVIDANDMARTIN.COM

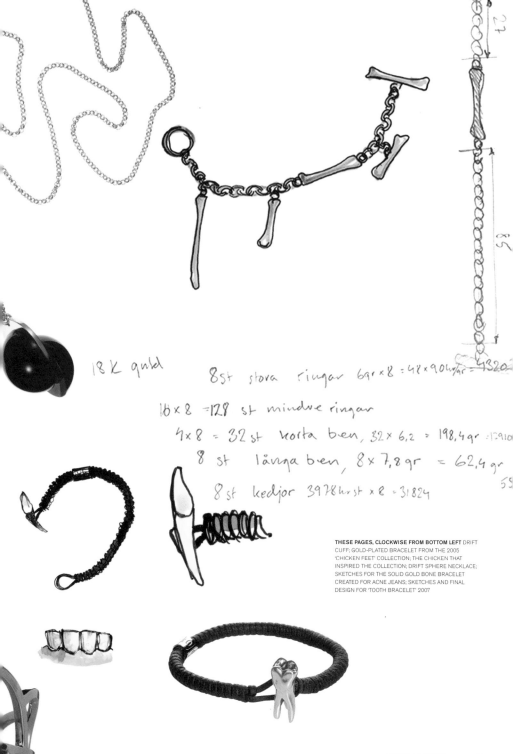

18 K guld

8st stora ringar 6gr×8 = 48×90kr/gr = 4320

16×8 =128 st mindre ringar

4×8 = 32st korta ben, 32×6,2 = 198,4gr =12910

8 st långa ben, 8×7,8gr = 62,4 gr

8st kedjor 3978kr/st ×8 = 31824   55

THESE PAGES, CLOCKWISE FROM BOTTOM LEFT DRIFT
CUFF; GOLD-PLATED BRACELET FROM THE 2005
'CHICKEN FEET' COLLECTION; THE CHICKEN THAT
INSPIRED THE COLLECTION; DRIFT SPHERE NECKLACE;
SKETCHES FOR THE SOLID GOLD BONE BRACELET
CREATED FOR ACNE JEANS; SKETCHES AND FINAL
DESIGN FOR 'TOOTH BRACELET' 2007

Delfina Delettrez

AS A FOURTH-GENERATION MEMBER OF THE FENDI DYNASTY
DELFINA DELETTREZ SEEMED DESTINED FOR A LIFE AS A FASHION
DESIGNER. INSTEAD, AGED NINETEEN AND RELUCTANT TO REST ON
THE FAMILY LAURELS, SHE FOUNDED A JEWELLERY LABEL AND
BEGAN SELLING HER 'MINI SCULPTURES, GOOD LUCK CHARMS AND
TALISMANS' FROM A NINETEENTH-CENTURY ROMAN PHARMACY.

When Delfina Delettrez launched her
jewellery line in 2007 it was to a flurry
of press speculation as to what a scion of
the Fendi family would unveil. Despite the
unprecedented amount of attention leveled
at her fledgling label Delettrez took it
in her stride. She was, after all, scarcely
a newcomer to the business. Her father,
the French jeweller Bernard Delettrez, had
worked in the industry for over 30 years
and it was while playing in his workshop
as a child that the seeds of her future
career were sewn. The turning point came
when she discovered among her father's
precious stones a red sapphire which he
set in a ring for her. 'It was a simple ring
but it was very significant to me,' she says.
'It was the first ring I ever had.'

Drawn to all things otherworldly
Delettrez channels a fascination with
magic and mysticism into her work. For
her debut range she drew on the fairytales
of her childhood to produce a collection
brimming with frogs, skulls, crowns,
flowers, fierce animals and poisonous
insects. Unorthodox materials – Tuscan
marble, Capodimonte ceramics, exotic
woods, chamois strips, bone and Murano
glass – overlaid with vividly coloured
wet-look varnishes ensure that, although
small, her pieces are full of captivating
detail. When asked what her father thinks
of his protégée's work Delettrez says:
'at the beginning he saw the skulls and
because his own work is so classical he
was worried. Now he loves it because
he understands my taste.'

To mark the collection's debut at Colette,
Delettrez commissioned her friend, the
actress Asia Argento, to write and direct
a short film called *Delfinasia*. The movie,
a dreamlike tale filled with the symbolism
that infused her collection, featured a heavily
pregnant Delettrez and her younger sister
at La Canonica – the rural family home
that inspires much of her work.

PREVIOUS PAGE FUR BRACELET FROM DELFINA DELETTREZ'S AW09 COLLECTION
ABOVE SPECTACLES DESIGNED BY DELFINA DELETTREZ FOR ALAIN MIKLI SS09

In 2008 Delettrez opened her first boutique in what had previously been an ancient pharmacy. Located in Rome's historic centre she wanted the tiny store to feel like a witch's house 'as a tribute to the herbs, tonics and poisons that were once sold there'. She sourced absinthe-green display cases and nineteenth-century pharmacy furnishings, and since her debut collection comprised 185 unique pieces which had taken 185 days to produce, Delettrez commissioned 185 small drawers to be made and finished each one with a handle unearthed in the neighbourhood's old tool shops.

Delettrez takes particular pride in having her pieces handmade by artisans who use antique jewellery techniques and whose workshops can be found in the streets around her boutique. Her ss09 collection, the aptly named Delirium, was a case in point. Keen to create the illusion of movement in her pieces, Delettrez charged the craftsmen with producing articulated jewellery in which unclasped stones created a sense of movement inside tiny enamelled eyes and mouths. 'These Roman streets are still full of many precious craftsmen's shops,' she says of the men who craft her jewellery. 'I am proud and honoured to be part of their world and they enjoy the work I ask them to do because it's different to what they are used to.'

To say that Delettrez grew up in rarefied fashion circles is to understate the point. With the Fendi name came a social circle that included family friend Karl Lagerfeld. Her logo – a crescent moon and five stars forming a D – was originally designed by Lagerfeld for her father in the 80s. But while adamant she will never work with Fendi (she refuses to use the name in a professional capacity) other ventures ensure she keeps a foot firmly in fashion's door. To date these have included a collaboration with Italian glovemakers Causse, for whom she created four exclusive fingerless glove styles, and a range of sunglasses for Alain Mikli. In both cases the accessories were embellished with trinkets and charms from her mainline collection.

When asked who she might like to collaborate with next, or what the future holds, Delettrez is easy-going: 'I don't like to make rigid plans. My mother advised me to find a job that I loved so that I would be happy and that's exactly what I did. For me this is a game and a pleasure and for now that's all I need.'

WWW.DELFINADELETTREZ.COM

A collection brimming with frogs, skulls, crowns, flowers, fierce animals and poisonous insects...

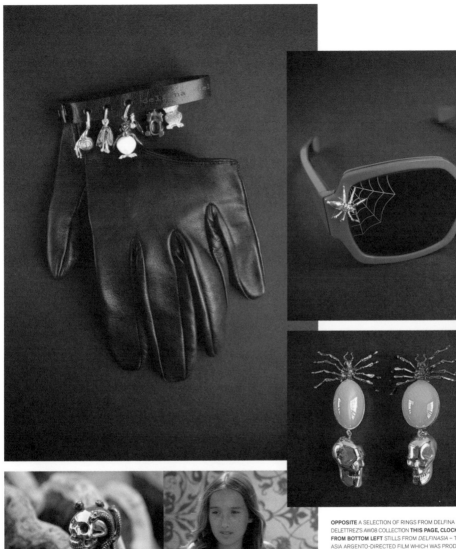

OPPOSITE A SELECTION OF RINGS FROM DELFINA DELETTREZ'S AW08 COLLECTION **THIS PAGE, CLOCKWISE FROM BOTTOM LEFT** STILLS FROM *DELFINASIA* – THE ASIA ARGENTO-DIRECTED FILM WHICH WAS PRODUCED TO MARK THE LAUNCH OF DELFINA'S DEBUT COLLECTION; ONE OF FOUR 'JEWEL GLOVES' STYLES DESIGNED BY DELETTREZ FOR ITALIAN GLOVE-MAKERS CAUSSE. EACH STYLE WAS EMBELLISHED WITH A SELECTION OF QUIRKY FIGURINES FROM HER MAINLINE JEWELLERY COLLECTION AND THE RANGE WAS UNVEILED AT COLETTE DURING PARIS' HAUTE COUTURE WEEK IN JULY 2008; SPECTACLES DESIGNED BY DELFINA DELETTREZ FOR ALAIN MIKLI SS09; EARRINGS FROM THE AW09 COLLECTION

Elke Kramer

ONE-WOMAN CREATIVE DYNAMO, ELKE KRAMER, LISTS GRAPHIC DESIGN, ILLUSTRATION, ART DIRECTION, FASHION TEXTILES AND FLOWER PICKING AMONG HER SKILLS. SHE ALSO LIKES TO GET EXPERIMENTAL IN THE KITCHEN 'BY COMBINING THE MOST UNLIKELY INGREDIENTS WITH PASSIONATE DEDICATION'. MUCH THE SAME MIGHT BE SAID OF HER APPROACH TO MAKING JEWELLERY.

Elke Kramer says she was always ambitious. 'I thought I could do everything. For me different media are like alternate outlets for ideas and I like to think I can add my touch to almost everything so that it becomes a part of my total creative vision.' It's a can-do attitude she attributes to her mother. 'I inherited her creative confidence and unbridled approach. Whether she was painting enormous murals, making ceramics or sewing quilts she showed me that when you're an artist or designer everything you touch becomes your art.'

After graduating from Sydney's College of Fine Arts in 2001 Kramer launched *Lilacmenace* – an experimental magazine with a fashion/art/music slant. Design jobs with Australian fashion labels, including Sass & Bide, Ksubi and Josh Goot, followed but it was a collaboration with Sydney-based designer Michelle Robinson in 2004 that marked Kramer's first foray into jewellery. 'It was so great to produce work in a new aesthetic that I wouldn't naturally have

gravitated towards,' says Kramer of the collection she created for Robinson's catwalk debut. 'I felt like I really got an opportunity to showcase my versatility as a designer.' As orders for Kramer's jewellery started to come in, and press interest was raised, Kramer seized the opportunity and added Elke Jewellery to her stable of business ventures.

In the wake of this success Kramer started designing bespoke collections to accompany the catwalk shows of Australian designer Jessie Hill. For Hill's Artificial Vs Real ss08 collection Kramer conceived a range of oversized hexagonal bangles with the objective of creating dramatic silhouettes on the runway. At around the same time she was commissioned by the Australian chain store Sportsgirl to make a diffusion collection of multicoloured resin bracelets, rings and leather goods, which were a sell-out success.

Explaining the source of her indefatigable drive Kramer says that she loves nothing

better than being briefed on a new project and letting her mind run wild. 'I also relish the opportunities to work with different people and get excited about what I can bring to the project. It opens me to new ideas and approaches.' Asked to explain the burgeoning reputation of Australia's fashion scene, she offers: 'I feel that young designers in Australia are so removed from other cultures and traditions that we can create in a very free and uncompromising way.'

When it comes to designing her own line each season Kramer sets herself a challenge – to explore new production techniques and work with hitherto unused materials. 'Much as I love collaborating, working on my own is my opportunity to be totally self-indulgent and experimental. Not having to compromise or adapt my visions – that's really fulfilling.'

And what visions they are. When she's not making quilted collars and beaded neckpieces inspired by architectural plans for Indian palaces, she might be slicing

graphic shapes from wood, or laser-cutting them from engraved acrylic, before bonding them to the kind of laminate more often seen on kitchen cabinets. The kooky experiments continue as Kramer moulds these unique building blocks into abstract flower petals, bugs and Aztec motifs that are in turn assembled into fan-shaped necklaces, bold bangles and statement-making earrings.

The need to maintain high levels of craftsmanship and durability while working with new materials means that Kramer is on a constant learning curve, sometimes finding things out the hard way. 'I'm always having to learn about the limitations of the materials I'm working with. Resin, for example, looks really solid and sturdy but is more like ceramic or glass in terms of brittleness. It can break if dropped or knocked against a hard surface so joins must be solid and weak points have to be avoided. Wearing samples myself helps me pick up on potential issues but I'm always terrified I will produce a large run of

something without noticing a design fault and have 100 pieces returned.' To date, Kramer says her worst nightmare hasn't come true.

To relieve the pressure of her hectic schedule Kramer indulges her homebody tendencies: 'I enjoy swimming and baking – if I wasn't involved with jewellery or design I could forge a career as a modern-day Martha Stewart and my friends can testify to my obsessions with my plants, DIY home crafts and nail art. But with her keen eye for image-making Kramer has less easy-going ideas on how her jewellery should be worn: 'My designs are not subtle so they need to be worn with poise and assurance. They need to be worn proudly.' Interestingly, she is less concerned with whether people find her work beautiful in the conventional sense: 'Beauty is subjective – originality is key to what I do. And anyway, I like the ambiguity of things being both beautiful and unattractive at the same time. I like that about all things in life.' WWW.ELKEKRAMER.COM

'Beauty is subjective – originality is key to what I do. And anyway, I like the ambiguity of things being both beautiful and unattractive at the same time. I like that about all things in life.'

PREVIOUS PAGE A MODEL WEARS JEWELLERY FROM ELKE KRAMER'S 'MIRACLES AND WONDER' COLLECTION SS09 **OPPOSITE** 'HOLLOW MORN' BRACELETS FROM THE 'ARTIFICIAL VS REAL' SS09 COLLECTION DESIGNED BY ELKE FOR JESSIE HILL **THIS PAGE, CLOCKWISE FROM LEFT** A MODEL WEARS BRACELETS FROM THE 'ARTIFICIAL VS REAL' SS09 COLLECTION DESIGNED BY ELKE FOR JESSIE HILL; NECKLACE FROM KRAMER'S OWN 'TROMPE L'OEIL' SS09 COLLECTION; CANDYASS NECKLACE FROM THE 'EXHALTATION OF SKYLARKS' SS05 COLLECTION

Erickson
Beamon

'LIKE ALL GREAT DESIGN ORIGINALS, ERICKSON BEAMON'S JEWELS OF FANTASY HOLD A MIRROR UP TO THEIR TIMES. AND WHAT TIMES THEY HAVE BEEN! – THE ROLLICKING, CORUSCATING, DANGEROUS 80S, THE SLEEK, SPARE, BARELY THERE 90S, AND OUR ECLECTIC NEW CENTURY: A JEWEL-BOX BRIMMING WITH MORE POSSIBILITIES...' HAMISH BOWLES IN AMERICAN *VOGUE*.

The day that Karen Erickson and Vicki Beamon decide to publish their memoirs is the day they'll have a best-seller on their hands. Their story reads like a been there, done that, got the designer T-shirt romp through three decades of style and their list of collaborators like a who's who of fashion's über-elite.

As in all the best tales this one begins with a friendship between two girls who left home in pursuit of a dream. Vicki Beamon takes up the story: 'When we met back in Detroit we were both really into music, the arts and, of course, fashion – Karen had a shoe shop that stocked the most amazing Terry de Havilland shoes. In 1982 we moved to Manhattan and fell straight into the whole Studio 54 scene where pretty soon we began to make friends and contacts.'

It was while working on designer Robert Molnar's catwalk show that the Erickson Beamon seeds were sown. 'Including Maripol you could count the jewellers in New York on one hand back then and as we couldn't find what we wanted we decided to make our own jewellery,' explains Beamon. 'We strung some crystals and beads on suede and that was it. We persuaded our friends at *Interview* magazine to let us place an advert and the first call we got was from Bergdorf Goodman with an order.'

Fast-forward to the present day and Erickson Beamon are second to none on the list of designer fashion jewellers. In addition to producing their own-name lines they have collaborated with numerous major designers over the years: Dries Van Noten, Dior, Ungaro, Anna Sui, Givenchy, Alexander McQueen, Anna Molinari, Calvin Klein, Donna Karan, Jil Sander, John Galliano, Marc Jacobs, Oscar de la Renta, Olivier Theyskens, Rifat Ozbek, Roberto Cavalli, Roland Mouret, Todd Lynn... Unsurprisingly, when they won the Best Catwalk Jewels category at the 2008 UK

Jewellery Awards it was for their 'ability to make an impact on the fashion runway.'

In 1985 Beamon relocated to London to set up the company's European branch. Ten years later she opened the Erickson Beamon boutique beneath which a higgledy-piggledy warren of workshops serves the UK operation's nerve centre. It is from here that Beamon continues to design for European commissions while the States-based Erickson takes care of the US. 'After all these years we still work really well together. I think the reason for that is we compete with each other. Karen's work is really good so naturally mine has to be better.'

Healthy competition may spur them on but it's the duo's intuition for fashion, from street style to haute couture, that has kept them at the top of their game. 'Our speciality is that we can do different methods of jewellery-making: macramé, beading, plastic, soldering. What puts the soul into the jewellery is that it's all handmade; it's couture.' Also key to their longevity has been a willingness to embrace new projects across the fashion spectrum. In addition to consultancy and private commissions they have put their name to lines for Debenhams in the UK and Target in the US and in June 2008 they made a collection of bejewelled plastic trinkets for Urban Outfitters. At the other end of the scale, the launch of Erickson Beamon Diamonds has seen them enter the fine jewellery arena which, says Beamon, has been like going back to school: 'Erickson Beamon designer jewellery is instant gratification, but the process for one of those diamond pieces takes around a year so we've been learning a lot of new lessons.'

Far from struggling to come up with new ideas after so long in the business, however, Beamon says quite the opposite is true. 'I have a constant flow of ideas and

PREVIOUS PAGE, LEFT THIS IMAGE APPEARED IN *NUMERO* MAGAZINE AS PART OF THE 'INNOCENCE' STORY. THE SHOOT WAS CONCEIVED AS AN HOMAGE TO ERICKSON BEAMON AND TO SHOWCASE THEIR AW08 JEWELLERY COLLECTION PREVIOUS PAGE, RIGHT LARGE-SCALE, ORNATELY BEADED JEWELLERY SUCH AS THE NECKPIECE SHOWN HERE IS A CLASSIC ERICKSON BEAMON SIGNATURE THESE PAGES, CLOCKWISE FROM LEFT ERICKSON BEAMON HAVE CREATED CATWALK JEWELLERY FOR AN IMPRESSIVE ROSTER OF FASHION DESIGNERS. EARRINGS FOR ZAC POSEN SS09; NECKLACES FOR ANNA SUI AW09; A TRIBAL-INSPIRED NECKPIECE AT ANNA SUI SS09; NECKLACE PRODUCED IN COLLABORATION WITH ETHICAL JEWELLERY COMPANY MADE

THIS PAGE, FROM LEFT A FEATHER NECKLACE BY ERICKSON BEAMON FOR EMMANUEL UNGARO AW99; NECKLACE DETAILS FROM THE 'DIAMONDS BY ERICKSON BEAMON' LINE; FOR SS09 ERICKSON BEAMON COLLABORATED WITH ETHICAL JEWELLERY BRAND, MADE, TO CREATE A LIMITED EDITION RANGE OF BEADED JEWELLERY; ERICKSON BEAMON-DESIGNED JEWELLERY AT JAEGER LONDON'S SS09 CATWALK SHOW OPPOSITE CUBE NECKLACE AND BUTTERFLY EARRINGS DESIGNED BY ERICKSON BEAMON FOR URBAN OUTFITTERS SS08

Their story reads like a been there, done that, got the designer T-shirt romp through three decades of style and their list of collaborators like a who's who of fashion's über-elite.

the trick is to keep them honed, if anything it's about keeping them in check.'

Each season Erickson Beamon produce somewhere in the region of ten collections and enough jewellery to cram Aladdin's cave full of iridescent leather cuffs, fruit-inspired clusters of semi-precious stones, heavy gold fringing, cascading ropes of coloured pearls, knotted silk ribbons and pendants dripping with jewels. With so much to choose from, pinpointing an Erickson Beamon signature is tricky, but heavily beaded necklaces, flamboyant chandelier earrings and crystal-encrusted cuffs are staples that undergo seasonal reinvention. Despite

the fabulously fake nature of their jewels Beamon is clear that what they produce is not costume jewellery: 'Costume is a term started in the 1920s and jewellery has moved so far along since then. Our jewellery's not designed to look real – we create fantasies that I'd refer to as designer fashion jewellery.'

Beamon is aware that the success she has enjoyed is down to a lot of hard work and a dash of luck: 'I'm so blessed that every day is creative. It's not easy and I'll never be a millionaire but I certainly have some great stories to tell. It's tough and I tell anyone who leaves us that.' Far from being turned off, however, Beamon's

protégés, including jeweller Scott Wilson, have gone on to forge their own successful careers and say they have a lot to thank Beamon for.

It's a sentiment echoed by one of Erickson Beamon's legion of fans, fashion designer Antonio Berardi, who has compared collaborating with them thus: 'It's like finding a golden ticket in one of Willy Wonka's chocolate bars. A truly magical experience where delicious, mouth-watering confections of all things precious are literally blown together, forming the most exquisite of trinkets that intoxicate the senses and leave you craving more.'

WWW.ERICKSONBEAMON.COM

Florian

FROM SIMPLE BEADED NECKLACES TO SCULPTURAL VACUUM-MOULDED BODY PIECES, FLORIAN'S JEWELLERY COMBINES HUMOUR, PHILOSOPHY AND EROTICISM. AN INTELLIGENTLY NUANCED APPROACH TO HIS CRAFT HAS LED TO HIGHLY ACCLAIMED COLLABORATIONS WITH EQUALLY CEREBRAL DESIGNERS HUSSEIN CHALAYAN AND COMME DES GARÇONS. JUST DON'T ASK HIM TO EXPLAIN WHAT IT ALL MEANS...

When he graduated from Vienna's University of Applied Arts with a specialism in advanced metal design Florian Ladstätter was intent on a career as an art jeweller. It wasn't long, however, before the limitations of getting his work into galleries and selling it to an elite sphere of specialists made it clear to Ladstätter that he needed a new direction and audience.

Florian's epiphany came in 2001. While preparing an exhibition he cast a series of coloured plastic pendants in epoxy resin. They were fresh and exciting but entirely unsuitable for a gallery environment. Fashion seemed the logical arena so Florian (for professional purposes he uses his first name only) set about altering his approach to design, creating jewellery that, in some cases, worked on a more subconscious level by 'altering the status quo in a subtle way'.

Despite the change of milieu, however, Florian's predilection for statement-making jewellery persisted and, by his own admission, this hangover from his art days resulted in work that continued to veer 'from easy wearing to weird sculpture.' He justifies the dichotomy thus: 'For use in the real world jewellery needs simply to be present somewhere at the edge of consciousness, enriching a situation in a subtle way through a touch of glamour, wit or even irritation. For a catwalk show or to create an editorial image, however, it needs to make an impact.'

As befits a man who studied philosophy for two years, Florian thinks a lot about his work. The paradox is that while he has firm ideas of what jewellery should, and shouldn't, be he objects to people's desire to attach specific meaning to it. 'I explore concepts but avoid definitive conceptual content that people are obliged to decode when they should simply enjoy the design. Aesthetic experience is a spontaneous process so I want my work to fuel the wearer's own fantasies rather than impose my own. And anyway, to dismiss great aesthetic possibilities for a poor conceptual gag makes no sense to me.'

Florian's wide-ranging inspirations veer from pop culture to high art; tribal decoration and Tsarist Russia to ocean cruises and the musings of the Marquis de Sade. Far from being literal interpretations, however, his designs are more about his fantasies of a place and people than the reality. 'My approach is not to consciously develop something out of my experiences but to let it all combine until some gut reaction fires my imagination.'

Starting with materials – fur, metal, crystal, plastics, cord, wood or leather – he arranges them (sometimes leaving them for up to a week) until it's clear which materials, shapes, colours and scales provide the greatest tension. 'Combining, say, cheap wooden beads with sparkling crystal on a necklace gives it energy and keeps it challenging and vibrant.' The next stage is to 'upload' the collection into his consciousness in order to balance each style within it.

To look at Florian's body of work over the years it is clear that jewellery's inherent sensuality is something that preoccupies him. The more elaborate versions of his multi-stranded bead necklaces and adjustable rope jewellery hint at bondage, while fleshy-looking tumescences moulded from shiny plastic provoke repulsion and fascination in equal measure. In March 07 Florian unveiled an 'erotically charged' collection of jewellery and surreal domestic objects that embodied these ideas. First displayed as a window installation at Colette he later re-contextualized the project, combining his work with the exhibits at Vienna's Museum of Applied Arts. In juxtaposing these objects from different periods and cultures his aim was to evoke different relations and associations. Appropriately, one of the tableaux featured an ivory cup depicting

'Aesthetic experience
is a spontaneous process
so I want my work to fuel
the wearer's own fantasies
rather than impose my own.'

PREVIOUS PAGE 'BEADS' CREATED AS A SPECIAL EDITION PROJECT FOR LONDON'S B STORE AND LES DEUX POISSONS GALLERY, TOKYO 2005 OPPOSITE A VACUUM-MOULDED RESIN FORMATION IS INCORPORATED INTO A SUPERSIZED NECKLACE BACKGROUND NECKLACES FROM COLLECTION CREATED BY FLORIAN FOR COMME DES GARÇONS' DOVER STREET MARKET STORE, AW08 THIS PAGE FOR AW07 FLORIAN UNVEILED 'LES FLEURS DU MAL' – A COLLECTION OF EROTICALLY CHARGED JEWELLERY AND SURREAL DOMESTIC OBJECTS. THESE IMAGES ARE TAKEN FROM A SHOOT CALLED 'THE SHAPE OF DESIRE', WHICH RAN IN THE LIMITED-EDITION CATALOGUE THAT WAS PRODUCED TO ACCOMPANY THE COLLECTION

THIS PAGE, CLOCKWISE FROM BOTTOM LEFT A DETAIL SHOT FROM THE 'SEASIDE SUMMER' COLLECTION SS09; IN 2005 FLORIAN TOOK A SELECTION OF HIS WORK TO TOKYO AND ASKED KIDS IN THE STREET TO MODEL HIS JEWELLERY IN THE WAY THEY FELT BEST SUITED IT. HERE A BOY WEARS THE 'SOMETHING BIOLOGICAL' BROOCH 2001; 'ENHANCERS' – A COLLECTION OF PINS CREATED FOR THE LIFE BALL AIDS CHARITY EVENT IN 2008 **OPPOSITE, ABOVE** A PASSERBY IN TOKYO STRIKES A POSE IN A PIECE FROM FLORIAN'S 2001 COLLECTION, **OPPOSITE, BELOW** A DETAIL SHOT FROM THE 'SEASIDE SUMMER' COLLECTION SS09

a Greek bacchanal with a dildo-like chrome pendant on a pink pearl string.

Asked, in the light of such projects, if he misses the art jewellery scene, Ladstätter says not. 'I work fast and have lots of ideas so I'm suited to fashion and to developing twice-yearly collections. And, for me, it's much smarter to create something that somebody else will complete by putting it into use. I think that's the difference. Most artists will not allow other people to finish their work.' The change of scene has been an auspicious one with high-profile projects following in its wake. In recent years he has produced two collections of his multi-stranded jewellery for Comme des Garçons and he was behind the headline-hitting acrylic bubble and beaded dresses that made such an impression on Hussein Chalayan's ss07 catwalk.

For shoe company Repetto he produced a special-edition ballet pump embellished with eruptions of silver beads and in 2008 he designed a collection of 2,000 injection-moulded badges as a VIP giveaway for the Life Ball AIDS charity event. As a designer more used to creating a limited number of pieces each season, Florian says this experience of producing jewellery in high volume was exciting because it allowed him to offer high-quality jewellery that was affordable to everybody and which, most importantly, still managed to appear 'quite erotic.'
WWW.FLORIAN-DESIGN.COM

OPPOSITE THE 'BUBBLE DRESS' DESIGNED BY FLORIAN FOR HUSSEIN CHALAYAN'S SS07 CATWALK SHOW DEMONSTRATED THE WAY FLORIAN IS ABLE TO EXTEND HIS JEWELLERY AESTHETIC INTO OTHER AREAS OF FASHION **THIS PAGE, LEFT** 'BEADS' CREATED AS A SPECIAL-EDITION PROJECT FOR LONDON'S B STORE AND LES DEUX POISSONS GALLERY, TOKYO 2005; **THIS PAGE, ABOVE** FLORIAN'S 'CONCEPTUAL NEOBAROQUE' LIMITED-EDITION BALLET PUMP DESIGNED FOR REPETTO SS09

' For use in the real world jewellery needs simply to be present somewhere at the edge of consciousness, enriching a situation in a subtle way through a touch of glamour, wit or even irritation. For a catwalk show or to create an editorial image, however, it needs to make an impact.'

Husam
el Odeh

HUSAM EL ODEH WAS A SUCCESSFUL ARTIST IN HIS NATIVE GERMANY UNTIL AN URGE TO EXPLORE NEW TERRITORY LED HIM TO SWAP BERLIN FOR LONDON AND FINE ART FOR FASHION JEWELLERY. DESPITE THE DIFFICULT DEADLINES, SLEEPLESS NIGHTS AND BLEEDING FINGERS THAT ARE PAR FOR THE COURSE IN HIS NEW JOB, HE SAYS HE WOULDN'T HAVE IT ANY OTHER WAY.

Husam el Odeh describes his shift from fine art to jewellery as a change of context rather than content. His work still focuses on the re-imagining of everyday objects in relation to the human body; jewellery, particularly in the arena of fashion, simply allows him to link the two more directly.

Giving shape to his ideas el Odeh presents symbols associated with man's cultural evolution in such a way as to render them ultimately meaningless in anything other than a decorative context: coins are strung together on necklaces; a crystal decanter bottle top cast in brass and suspended on a chain is pleasantly weighty but ultimately redundant. His favourite motif is the iconic Smiley: 'It's the easiest depiction of a human face. Just two dots and a line and each time you get a slightly different emotion. It's all about how we perceive it.'

Much of el Odeh's design process is intuitive to the point of being random but, he says, his goal is to make people stop and think: 'If one of my pieces manages to make one person realize there might be another way of looking at the smallest detail I would consider it a success.' Using wool, wood, fabric, leather, latex and metal el Odeh pares his work right down. With inspirations including nineteenth-century poetry, disused buildings, surreal music videos, Stone Age tools and the work of German installation artist Rebecca Horn, it's no surprise his work can appear a touch austere. 'I tend to make quite stern, masculine jewellery – my ethos is very German in that respect – but by putting

it on a female body an interesting visual tension is created and the pieces take on new meaning.'

If a picture paints a thousand words then a visit to el Odeh's east London studio tells an interesting story. On one side a workbench is strewn with the flotsam and jetsam of his street finds: watch pieces, beads, crystals, coins, tool bits, a green plastic spider ring. 'I need all this stuff,' explains el Odeh. 'I can't create without it and I love experimenting and seeing where things will go. I find that the happy accident can be a springboard into really interesting territory.' On the opposite side of the studio finished pieces are displayed ready for visitors to try them out: how a piece feels is as important as how it looks so passing the touch test is essential.

After graduating with a degree in jewellery design from Middlesex University el Odeh was quick to infiltrate London's fashion scene. Sponsorship from talent-spotting initiative Fashion East and the British Fashion Council enabled him to exhibit his work at London Fashion Week and he has also undertaken a series of collaborative ventures with fashion designers whose approach and aesthetics resonate with his own. The most high profile of these has been an ongoing partnership with London's king of cling, Marios Schwab. 'Marios has a highly sophisticated understanding of the body and strikes an elegant balance between tender, sexual and empowered,' says el Odeh. 'We have developed an intense and finely tuned dialogue, where I interpret

'I love the way
fashion can, on the
surface, pretend to
be important, but
retains a certain
irony about its
own function.'

PAGE 74 & PAGE 75, LEFT COMB-INSPIRED PIECES DESIGNED BY HUSAM EL ODEH FOR MIHARA YASUHIRO'S AW07 PARIS MENSWEAR SHOW BLUR THE BOUNDARY BETWEEN JEWELLERY AND HEADWEAR PAGE 75, RIGHT WORK IN PROGRESS IN EL ODEH'S STUDIO PREVIOUS PAGE CLOCKWISE FROM LEFT THIS IMAGE SHOWING ONE OF EL ODEH'S SIGNATURE COMB PIECES FEATURED ON THE COVER OF TANK MAGAZINE; STROBE PENCIL NECKLACE DESIGNED FOR SIV STØLDAL'S 'COVER UP' MENSWEAR SHOW AW07; IMAGE FROM THE SUMMER 06 ISSUE OF CENT MAGAZINE FEATURING EL ODEH'S 'DOUBLE CLOCK DIAL' NECKLACE THIS PAGE A SELECTION OF SHOTS TAKEN IN HUSAM EL ODEH'S LONDON-BASED STUDIO WHERE PIECES ARE DISPLAYED IN SUCH A WAY THAT VISITORS ARE ENCOURAGED TO TOUCH AND INTERACT WITH THEM

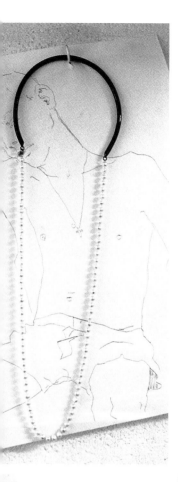

his approach into my specific materials.' In literal terms this has seen him extend his jewellery aesthetic into pieces including the armour-like metal plates that embellished the body conscious dresses of Schwab's aw07 collection and a limited edition spin-off line for Marios Schwab for Topshop, the best-selling piece from which was an Alice band decorated with bolted-on metal panels.

For Swedish designer, Siv Støldal, el Odeh has designed three catwalk jewellery collections (including a range of violent-looking spiky pencil pendants) as well as a jewellery range for Støldal's TopMan line. He made the memorable chicken wire accessories for Ann-Sofie Back's ss07 catwalk collection and, as part of a long-standing professional relationship with Japanese designer Mihara Yasuhiro, he has created men's jewellery and accessories including a range of hairpieces moulded from highly polished silver combs. He even did his bit for charity in 2007 with a collection of pin-badges that were sold in TopMan to raise awareness about testicular cancer.

In fashion el Odeh seems to have found his spiritual home. 'Jewellery gives me a platform to interact with a wider audience,' he explains. 'What's more, I love the way fashion can, on the surface, pretend to be important, but retains a certain irony about its own function. I don't want to get too serious about things.'

Yet despite the obvious affection with which the fashion fraternity regards el Odeh he says his biggest buzz is getting compliments from people who don't necessarily work in the industry. 'I was on a plane wearing a VW-logo pin badge I'd designed and this guy started telling me how much he liked it and how it reminded him of being a kid. The subtexts and cultural references associated with that symbol resonated with him on a different level.' And that, says el Odeh, is why he has no regrets about leaving his old life behind: 'I love my work and even though sometimes I lose sleep over deadlines and I work so hard my fingers bleed, it's a privilege to be able to make a living out of something that makes each day exciting.'
WWW.HUSAMELODEH.COM

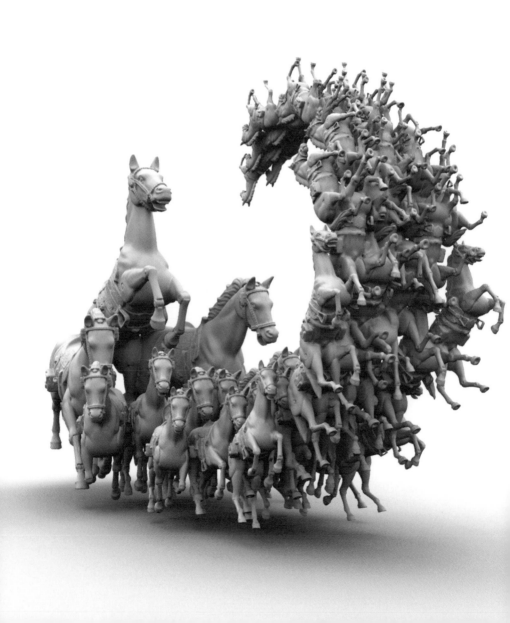

Jordan Askill

USING CLASSIC GOLDSMITHING TECHNIQUES TO REALIZE SCI-FI-INFLUENCED CONCEPTS JORDAN ASKILL PRODUCES BODIES OF WORK THAT EXPLORE HIS FASCINATION WITH METAMORPHOSIS. MUTATING CASTLES INTO SPACESHIPS OR A DOG'S FACE INTO A MOUNTAIN, HIS WORK EVOLVES THROUGH SEVERAL STAGES BEFORE IT BECOMES RECOGNIZABLE AS WEARABLE JEWELLERY.

There's a story Jordan Askill relates to underscore his fascination with an object's evolution. It involves a giant pearl – known as La Peregrina – which was originally owned by Henry VIII's daughter, Mary. Some 400 years later La Peregrina (which by then had been re-modelled by Cartier) fell into the hands of movie legend Elizabeth Taylor, where it remains to this day. 'I love the idea of that pearl being passed down through the generations and given a new lease of life so it became modern,' explains Askill. 'That's kind of how I want my jewellery to feel.'

The starting point for each of Askill's collections is always a found object that strikes a chord with the mood he's in at the time. With the help of British artist, Christopher Cornish, Askill has developed a technique that enables him to produce incredibly detailed silicone and resin

sculptures based on those random objects. The most remarkable of these so far is his Wave sculpture – a fractal-shaped form composed of dozens of horses, each one fractionally smaller than those preceding it.

It is only once the sculpture designs have been finalized that Askill begins to think about the jewellery which, although not a literal translation, resembles the sculpture in shape and mood. 'I go into more detail with the jewellery – which in effect becomes a wearable 3D-version of the sculpture – but conceptually the sculpture is the purer of the two stages. Together they tell a stronger story but the jewellery is the kind of thing that would inhabit a world where the sculptures could come to life' says Askill, seeking to explain how the two co-exist.

Askill's debut collection, unveiled in 2008, started life as a small plastic sword that inspired a sculpture of sword-wielding young knights that ultimately became a gold bird pendant. The rest of the collection included articulated rosebuds, a boy's head that opened to reveal a gemstone, and a swallow whose circular flight path was translated into a wrist-swooping gold cuff.

Although his materials and methods have their basis in fine jewellery Askill's impressive fashion pedigree has a profound bearing on his work and outlook. While studying fashion at East Sydney's TAFE he spent time as an intern with Alexander McQueen in London. On returning to Sydney to complete his degree he scooped the prize for fashion excellence at the end of year awards. Design work for Ksubi and his own ready-to-wear line followed before a serendipitous meeting with Hedi Slimane (who as the head of Dior Homme was guest-editing an issue of Australian *Vogue*) led to an offer of work experience which turned into an internship, then a full-time design job in Paris. The icing on the cake proved to be Askill's turn down the Dior Homme ss05 catwalk.

'In Paris I learned how important an understanding of culture is to the design process. I spent a lot of time visiting galleries, going to gigs, scouring the flea markets and marvelling at Versailles. It was all part of my cultural education,' says Askill of his twenty-first century Grand Tour. Sources of inspiration include Eutruscan craftspeople, jewellery of the late 1800s, the iconic Fabergé and mythological themes from Paolo Uccello's painting of Saint George and the Dragon. But in stark

contrast to this taste for antiquities, computer technology and science fiction hold him in thrall to their ultra-detailed approach which he channels in such a way that while his work references the past it also 'moves forward'.

When not making jewellery Askill has a successful sideline styling commercials and music videos with Collider – a collective of artists and film-makers headed by his elder brother Daniel – who have produced ad campaigns for the likes of Nike and Dior Fahrenheit 32. For friend and fellow jeweller Michelle Jank's ss08 fashion show he art-directed a video installation and, says Daniel, down the line they plan to produce a film in which Jordan's jewellery and sculptures will play a starring role.

In early 2009 Askill extended his collection to include a range of hand-carved rock crystal pieces for men, and his limited-edition jewellery is now stocked at Dover Street Market in London and Rik Owens' boutique in Paris. As his profile grows, and he gains an increasing foothold in the fashion arena, Askill is keen not to loose sight of what motivates him: 'Trends in fashion are important to me as part of the development of our time and I like to work with different techniques that have a relevance to the here-and-now. But, it's important for me to design as if I were writing a diary, so it's quite personal. Ultimately, what I want is to reflect my views and thoughts by creating images that are timeless and strike a chord with others.'
WWW.ASKILLPROJECTS.COM

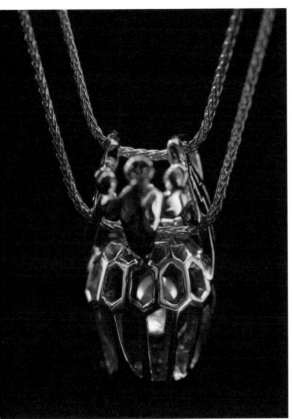

...articulated
rosebuds,
a boy's head
that opened
to reveal a
gemstone, and
a swallow whose
circular flight
path was
translated into
a wrist-swooping
gold cuff.

Judy Blame

AS A DENIZEN OF LONDON'S LEGENDARY 80S CLUB SCENE JUDY BLAME MADE A NAME FOR HIMSELF CREATING FOUND-OBJECT JEWELLERY PIECES FOR THE LIKES OF NENEH CHERRY AND BOY GEORGE. BLAZING A TRAIL THROUGH THREE DECADES OF UK FASHION, THE ELUSIVE BUT PROLIFIC BLAME HAS BECOME THE GO-TO GURU FOR A NEW GENERATION OF DESIGNERS LOOKING TO LEARN FROM A BRITISH STYLE ICON.

Was fashion always your passion?

I don't think I ever really had a career plan per se – I certainly never trained in the professional sense but when I ran away from home punk rock was in full swing so I developed that ethos of making and customizing my own clothes. By the time the New Romantic scene sprung up in the early 80s all us peacocks were creating looks to go with the music we were into. Many's the time I sat around with the likes of Stephen Jones, John Galliano and Antony Price planning that week's clubbing outfits.

What was the first piece of jewellery you made?

Me and my friend Scarlett couldn't afford a new outfit each time we went out so one night I made these necklaces from huge black beads and we wore them over some simple knee-length chemises. The next piece – which I called Dr Who – was made from a multicoloured ball of string with a few wooden beads on it. After that I started making jewellery from found objects and the idea just grew: buttons, string, safety pins, rubber bands, badges, feathers, champagne corks, paperclips, pill bottles, stamps – anything I could lay my hands on got incorporated. One of my first collections was made from bits of old clay pipe and bones I'd found on the river bank. I called it Father Thames.

'The English are a peacock nation. Just look at our influence on walking sticks, hats and club culture.'

What defines the Judy Blame aesthetic?

My work definitely has that British craft thing about it. Sewing, buttons, string, pins – I can make something from anything and I see beauty in everything, from industrial chains to a Coca-Cola can that's been run over by a car. When I'm collaborating I'll adapt each collection according to the designer I'm working with but they're all stamped with my anarchy. People know they're not going to get a couple of rows of beads off me.

Where do you find your materials?

All my original samples come from something I find. One of my favourite hunting grounds is The Palace of the Feathers in Brazil that supplies all the carnivals. It's five floors heaving with all sorts of chains, feathers, beads, buttons and baubles. I have to be careful with my excess luggage coming home.

What's the secret of your success?

I love teamwork – I'd rather get down on my hands and knees and start pinning than tell someone else what to do. Working with young designers keeps me excited too. I was really helped out when I was young so I enjoy passing that on. On another level, what I do has become relevant to the vogue for sustainable fashion. In the early 80s people thought I was mad with that whole scavenging and recycling thing but now designers like Noki (with whom I've collaborated) are working along very similar lines and making waves.

With which other new designers have you worked?

So many over the years, but of the current lot I've worked with Gareth Pugh for six seasons now and that includes making the jewellery for his debut menswear show in Paris. When we first met, Gareth asked me to adapt one of my signature styles, Stolen Property, for a show and things developed from there. Gareth still has the ability to shock and that's a rare thing in fashion today. For Giles' ss09 collection I reproduced laser-cut fabric bunny shapes in Perspex and built them up into these elaborate neck ruffs.

What was working with Comme des Garçons' Rei Kawakubo like?

I've always rated the Japanese for turning fashion on its head so I was thrilled when Rei Kawakubo invited me to work with her. When I did the jewellery for her ss05 Homme Plus show her brief was pretty succinct: 'pink and gold'. She didn't want me at the fittings and I never saw the clothes until the day of the show when I turned up with pink plastic toy soldiers and pompoms strung up on gold chains. That same year she commissioned me to design a range of jewellery and display it in a specially curated Judy Blame section at Comme's Dover Street Market.

How versatile is what you do?

Because of the way my jewellery's made it's an aesthetic that's very adaptable. When I'm styling a shoot I can extend the idea of embellishment to customize the clothes. When Marc Jacobs was designing Louis Vuitton's 2007 cruise collection he asked me to customize some LV-monogrammed denim. I designed a range of shorts, T-shirts, hats and bags covered with buttons, lace and clusters of hanging charms. I did some cute rubber boots for a Brazilian shoe brand called Melissa, too.

Why do you think so many fashion jewellers come out of the UK?

I don't know what it is about England but we've always been really good at accessories. Maybe it's down to the English sense of dressing up to be individual. We are a peacock nation. Just look at our influence on walking sticks, hats and club culture. You can do so much with the right accessory.

So, how important is jewellery in the grand scheme of things?

Look at a photo of Coco Chanel – you remember the pearl ropes and cuffs. In the same way, you remember Schiaparelli's buttons and her shoe hat. Accessories, and by extension jewellery, allow us to invent ourselves: they're the icing on the cake. That's why I always have been, and always will be, drawn to them.

THIS PAGE, CLOCKWISE FROM LEFT
JUDY BLAME DESIGNED THE JEWELLERY
FOR GARETH PUGH'S DEBUT MENSWEAR
SHOW AW09; A MODEL WEARS A PIECE
CREATED BY JUDY BLAME FOR DESIGNER
NOKI'S LABEL, NHS; A DESIGN FOR
GARETH PUGH'S SS08 CATWALK SHOW;
STILETTO HEEL CORSAGE FOR RICHARD
NICHOLL'S AW09 CATWALK SHOW;
SKETCHBOOK IDEAS FOR GARETH
PUGH'S AW09 MENSWEAR SHOW

LEFT THIS PHOTO, TAKEN IN JUDY BLAME'S WORKSPACE, SHOWS A CLASSIC BLAME DESIGN PACKED WITH FOUND OBJECTS, COLOUR, TEXTURE AND HUMOUR **ABOVE** FOR THE 2007 LOUIS VUITTON CRUISE COLLECTION MARC JACOBS COMMISSIONED BLAME TO CUSTOMIZE DENIM ACCESSORIES WITH HIS SIGNATURE JANGLES OF JEWELLERY **OPPOSITE** BUTTONS, BEADS AND SAFETY PINS ARE ASSEMBLED INTO AN EYE-CATCHING GOLD TRINKET

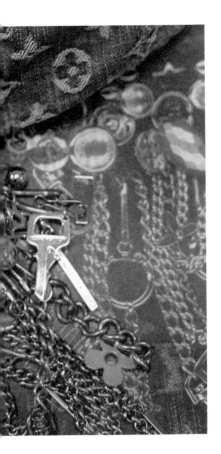

'One of my first collections was made from bits of old clay pipe and bones I'd found on the river bank. I called it Father Thames.'

Lara Bohinc

IN THE DECADE SINCE LARA BOHINC FOUNDED HER COMPANY HER NAME HAS BECOME SYNONYMOUS WITH GLAMOROUS JEWELLERY AND STATEMENT-MAKING ACCESSORIES. AS THE GO-TO DESIGNER FOR LUXURY BRANDS SEEKING TO CAPITALIZE ON HER CREATIVE CACHET SHE HAS BUILT AN IMPRESSIVE PORTFOLIO OF COLLABORATIONS BUT IT'S WITH HER OWN LINES THAT SHE PLANS TO CONQUER THE WORLD.

Lara Bohinc says that for as long as she can remember she wanted to study jewellery design. Thwarted by the lack of facilities to do so in her native Slovenia she opted instead for a degree in industrial design at the Ljubljana Academy of Fine Arts and made jewellery in her spare time. Her tenacity paid off and straight out of college she landed a postgraduate position to study jewellery design at London's Royal College of Art.

In 1997, with the ink still wet on her graduation certificate, Bohinc launched a line of jewellery and leather accessories under the moniker Lara Boeing 747 – a wry homage to the famous aeroplane and play on her own name. It wasn't long before her designs won a New Generation Design Award at London Fashion Week. Boeing, however, were less impressed and Lara was persuaded to re-brand her company as LB107 – the numerals this time alluding to the number on her hospital band when she was born. Today the name has changed once again, pared back to the gimmick-free Lara Bohinc International.

With hindsight, it is perhaps lucky that Bohinc was unable to study jewellery design when she wanted to because she has her industrial training to thank for her penchant for problem-solving and a curiosity about form and function that have become her signature. 'I'm a product designer, not a craftsperson so I'm much more interested in exploring new techniques', says Bohinc, who designs everything on a computer. 'My challenge is finding ways to economize in terms of cutting down on the number of steps it takes to create the desired end product. I'm interested in

structure and construction and working out a problem or puzzle. Some of the ideas I use in my jewellery have taken a long time to perfect.' Her famous rope-like jewellery is a case in point – she has spent years refining the links and clasps.

Her savvy business brain and eye for a winning design mean that Bohinc is never short of prospective partners to collaborate with. A glance at the profile section on her website reveals that in addition to an ongoing design consultancy role with Cartier International she has worked with an impressive roster of luxury fashion brands including Gucci, Costume National, Lanvin, Exte, Guy Laroche, Marcus Lupfer, Julien McDonald and Maria Chen. Many of these projects were, she says, for the catwalk but contracts prevent her divulging more. 'I enjoyed the work but the turnaround is so fast that I find I learn a lot more when I work on my own line,' is all

she will reveal. But despite her apparently no-nonsense approach Bohinc has a well-developed, if somewhat perverse, sense of humour that filters into works, such as the ornamental silver headphones she designed for a friend which fit over the ears but emit no sound or a Braille rubber choker and cuffs whose inverted 'Love is blind' messages made them illegible even to the blind.

Each season Bohinc designs her jewellery and accessories collections in tandem. Since these are often evolutions of previous season's ideas (variations on her best-selling item, the Solar Eclipse bracelet, have been in continuous production since 2007) she has built up an instantly recognizable body of work that is defined by signature motifs such as art deco-inspired scrolls, repeated geometric patterns, and knitted or knotted chains constructed from gold-plated and rhodium-finished brass.

Inspired by nature and architecture she says her aim is to, 'create objects that women like to wear and that are beautiful.' A devoted celebrity fanbase (Sadie Frost, Kate Moss, Cameron Diaz and Gwen Stefani have been snapped in Bohinc's bijoux) attest to her having achieved that ambition but, says Bohinc, spotting her work on someone in the street gives her the greatest kick: 'then I know they bought it because they love it not because a stylist told them to wear it.'

In 2008, to mark a decade in business, Bohinc added to her portfolio with a collection of fine jewellery and a stand-alone boutique on London's affluent Sloane Street. She says it's just the start: 'My aim is to extend the line to other products and open more shops internationally. That's the way to build a strong business. That's the key to global domination!'
WWW.LARABOHINC.COM

PREVIOUS PAGE AN ORNATE RING FROM LARA BOHINC'S 'SATURN HONEYCOMB' LINE SS09 **OPPOSITE** A MODEL SPORTS A CLASSIC BOHINC DESIGN RE-IMAGINED FOR SS08 **THIS PAGE, CLOCKWISE FROM ABOVE** SS09'S PEARL-EMBELLISHED 'COCO' COLLECTION INCLUDED RINGS SUCH AS THIS AND WAS INSPIRED BY THE BIRTH OF BOHINC'S FIRST CHILD, DAUGHTER COCO; 'SATURN HONEYCOMB' RING SS09; 'SATURN HONEYCOMB' BRACELET SS09; 'COCO' EARRINGS SS09; 'COCO' RING SS09; 'YUPANA' BRACELET SS09; 'COCO' BRACELET SS09

BELOW LAPIZ LAZULI 'SOLARIS' RING FROM BOHINC'S FINE JEWELLERY COLLECTION WHICH DEBUTED IN OCTOBER 2007 **OPPOSITE PAGE, CLOCKWISE FROM BOTTOM RIGHT** 'COCO' BRACELET 2009; 'SATURN HONEYCOMB' NECKLACE 2009; 'YUPANA' NECKLACE SS09; THIS DARK BRASS BRACELET IS A CLASSIC STYLE THAT IS REGULARLY REISSUED DUE TO ITS POPULARITY WITH BOHINC'S FANS

'Bohinc has a well-developed, if somewhat perverse, sense of humour that filters into works such as a Braille rubber choker and cuffs whose inverted "Love is blind" messages made them illegible even to the blind.'

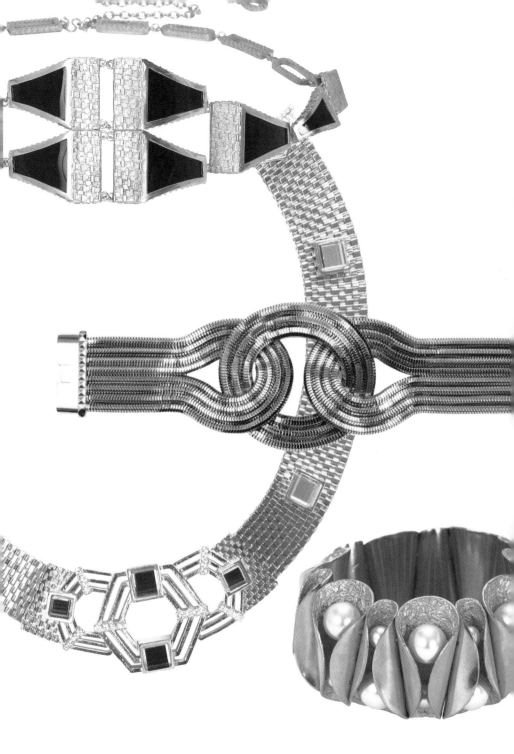

Laura B

LAURA BORTOLAMI DIDN'T LET LITTLE THINGS LIKE A LACK OF PROFESSIONAL TRAINING OR AN INABILITY TO DRAW STAND IN HER WAY WHEN SHE MADE THE DECISION TO BECOME A JEWELLERY DESIGNER. WITH HEAVYWEIGHT BEHIND-THE-SCENES FASHION EXPERIENCE AND AN ALREADY BULGING CONTACT BOOK, SUCCESS WAS ONLY A MATTER OF TIME.

It took a couple of career re-thinks and several changes of address before Laura Bortolami settled into what has become a very successful career. After graduating, the Italian native moved to Milan with every intention of becoming a translator. Her plans were sidetracked, however, when the offer of a job at Giorgio Armani's HQ came her way. Some time later, having caught the fashion bug, Bortolami moved on to an international sales position at Versace, and then a stint at Anna Molinari. She then moved to Dolce & Gabbana where she stayed for almost ten years. 'I've been lucky to learn the business side at such successful brands,' says Bortolami of the commercial skills she gained along the way. 'Selling, distribution, clients, how to conceive and create a collection – they've all been so useful when I set up my own company.'

In 1994, putting her business acumen and networking skills to work, she launched her jewellery and accessories label, Laura B. Under the name Laura B Collection Particulière she began to produce one-off pieces of jewellery constructed from antique beads, buckles and coins.

Bortolami's jewellery is best recognized by her signature metal mesh whose resemblance to chain mail imbues her work with an antique appearance. The effect is enhanced by details such as scrolling oak leaves fashioned into clasps and a sprinkling of pearls and semi-precious stones such as turquoise, onyx and fluorite. But if her work has a vintage feel, her approach is thoroughly modern: 'What I do is entirely fashion,' explains Bortolami of her market. 'It's not so much about the sculpture or the techniques, and it's not meant to be shown in a gallery. My concern is simply that the final object enhances someone's personal look and in that sense my jewellery is very close to the idea of an accessory in the shoe or bag tradition.' Her no-frills attitude has served her well and today Barcelona-based Bortolami presides over a successful international business selling to the clients she wooed back in her luxury brand days. Bortolami adopts a similarly fuss-free stance when it comes to designing. Throughout the year she researches materials: fabrics, chains, stones, buckles, even vintage brooches that she'll dismantle for a specific detail to be reproduced in silver later. She hides her treasures in the drawers of a large cabinet to which only she has access. 'I collect what I like and then at some point, perhaps years later, a particular piece becomes the thing on which a collection will hinge. I've tried to understand how it happens and the only way I can explain it is that my mood at that given moment will make the special piece sparkle before my eye in a way that it hasn't before.'

When the time comes to create a collection (she produces four a year: two women's and two men's) she lays everything on a table and begins to make combinations. As the direction becomes

'I collect what I like and then at some point, perhaps years later, a particular piece becomes the thing on which a collection will hinge.'

PREVIOUS PAGE, LEFT LAURA B'S
SIGNATURE MATERIAL IS A SPECIALLY
DEVELOPED METAL MESH OF THE KIND
USED TO CREATE THESE NECKLACES
FROM THE AW08 WOMEN'S COLLECTION
PREVIOUS PAGE, RIGHT ON HER TRAVELS
LAURA COLLECTS TRINKETS THAT CATCH
HER EYE. THESE SEA-THEMED ITEMS
INSPIRED THE MEN'S SS08 COLLECTION
THIS PAGE, CLOCKWISE FROM TOP 'MASAI'
NECKLACE AW07; 'SAVANA' THIN BRACELET
WITH A CROCODILE BACKSTRIP SS07; GREY
PEARL NECKLACE AW08

clearer she leaves the studio, often for a run, and this is when inspiration hits. Because of her lack of professional design training Bortolami works with two designers who assemble the work and because she doesn't draw she, and her jewellers and craftsmen, work directly on the mannequin.

In 2003 Bortolami launched Laura B for Men and each season both women's and men's collections share design details, the only difference says Bortolami, is that 'For my women's collections I design what I would desire; for men it's what I'd like my man to wear – although personally I think all a man really needs are cufflinks.'

With her reputation well and truly established Bortolami has started taking on bespoke commissions, including a range of men's and women's accessories for Jean Paul Gaultier, a selection of which appeared on his ss09 catwalk. In the wake of that project it was to Bortolami that Gaultier turned when he needed someone with know-how to realize a metal mesh and feather dress for an haute couture show. On adding yet another high-profile fashion name to her CV, Bortolami beams: 'I wanted to collaborate with a designer I really like, and I adore him, so it was just perfect really.'

WWW.LAURAB.INFO

ABOVE LAURA BORTOLAMI HIDES THE OBJECTS THAT SHE COLLECTS FOR INSPIRATION IN A LARGE CABINET TO WHICH ONLY SHE HAS ACCESS. WHEN THE TIME IS RIGHT PIECES SUCH AS THE ONES SHOWN HERE ARE TAKEN OUT AND INCORPORATED INTO THE CURRENT COLLECTION **OPPOSITE PAGE, CLOCKWISE FROM BOTTOM LEFT** 'ARROW' RINGS; MESH DETAIL; CHAIN DETAIL; BORTOLAMI SAYS SHE ALWAYS PREFERS TO DESIGN DIRECTLY ON THE STAND; MESH DETAIL

…her signature
is a metal mesh
whose resemblance
to chain mail
imbues the work
with an antique
appearance.

Ligia Dias

SWISS DESIGNER LIGIA DIAS MAKES IT HER BUSINESS TO EXPLORE THE 'JUXTAPOSITION OF BASIC RAW MATERIALS WITH THE BOURGEOIS VALUES OF LUXURY' THROUGH THE MEDIUM OF JEWELLERY. THE FRUITS OF THIS INTELLECTUAL QUEST ARE FABULOUS NECKLACES FILLED WITH COLOUR, TEXTURE AND IDIOSYNCRATIC CHARM.

It would be any fashion student's dream come true: a personal invitation from Alber Elbaz to join his team. That's what happened to Ligia Dias when, during a placement at Lanvin, she so impressed the legendary designer that the minute she finished her studies at Paris' Studio Berçot he opened a position for her in his Parisian atelier. Working on the womenswear collections, with the added responsibility of running the embroidery programme, Dias gained invaluable experience but, she says, what stood her in greatest stead were Elbaz's ideas about fashion: 'He taught me what luxury was. His obsessive quest for fashion that is both practical and luxurious chimed with my own philosophy and I rejoice in having learned from him.'

In 2005, with three years' experience at Lanvin behind her, Dias launched herself as an independent designer. Rather than fashion, however, she chose to specialize in jewellery, marking the move with the launch of Ligia Dias Colliers. It was a decision in no small part borne out of practical considerations. 'Jewellery was a form that fitted nicely onto the size of my bench when I didn't yet have a workshop. I invested very little money to produce my first collection and that is something I wouldn't have been able to do had I opted for garments.'

Early in her new career an exhibition of her work at the Centre Culturelle Suisse in Paris brought her to the attention of Comme des Garçons' creative director, Rei Kawakubo. In addition to buying Dias' work for Comme's international stores, Kawakubo commissioned her to produce a range of knitwear for the brand's aw06 retail collection. Applying her jewellery aesthetic to the garments she produced a collection of bejewelled cardigans and jumpers that were an instant hit.

With her profile raised, other projects followed. In March 2007 Dias was one of ten designers invited to produce a one-off necklace to mark the tenth anniversary celebrations of Parisian boutique Colette.

She designed a capsule jewellery collection for the 3:1 Philip Lim ss08 catwalk show, then in early 2009 she joined jewellers Florian and Scott Wilson in producing a limited edition pair of ballet pumps for the shoe company, Repetto. To accompany her embellished Electric Bourgeoisie shoes Dias also designed a subversive interpretation of the traditional pearl necklace.

The appropriation – or more specifically, misappropriation – of classic jewellery iconography is a subject on which Dias has very firm ideas: 'I feel that some of the jewellery world's most beautiful symbols are now used with so little consideration that they are in danger of becoming devalued.' The skull, she says, is a case in point. 'In recent years we have seen it too much in fashion jewellery, clothes, bags and even toilet paper. I don't think that customers, or even designers, know that it is part of our cultural and artistic heritage with a lot of meaning.' Dias herself admits to 'an obsession' with luxury jewellery motifs such as strings of pearls and faceted stones. The point, she says, is to use them with respect.

Dias' primary visual influences are Swiss graphic design, Bauhaus, modernism, Wiener Werkstätte and Russian constructivism. Her inspirations are less thematic, more a hybrid of ideas, colours and thoughts. 'I collect files full of images but I don't necessarily consult them when I'm making a collection. I work a lot from memory in a way that my jewellery pieces are an accumulation of ideas.'

In terms of style, Dias' work varies little from one season to the next, 'I come back to the same ideas season after season so I view my collections more as a work in progress.' Necklaces on the whole sit close to the neck, simpler models limited to a fuss-free row of beads, more elaborate versions resembling ornate bibs. Variety is introduced through her no-holds-barred mix of materials including, but by no means limited to, cords, curb chains, glass beads, Swarovski crystals, semi-precious stones, brass plates, Tyrolean ribbon, Palladium chains, leather strips, pearls, ostrich feather fringes, lambskin tassels and mink pompoms. It's the kind of jewellery that elicits a smile.

Her business now well established, Dias says she is keen to expand her repertoire: 'One needs to respond constantly to growing competition and to limit yourself to one thing has become less and less possible in the present climate.' Consequently, in 2009 she launched her first men's jewellery line. Comprising leather bracelets and unisex metal necklaces it was presented as a masculine translation of the mainline collection. 'For this first collection I wanted to accustom new clients to my classic components. Later I'd like to go further and experiment with more daring pieces.' Feather trims and fur pompoms for him could be just around the corner.
WWW.LIGIADIAS.COM

...a subversive interpretation of the traditional pearl necklace.

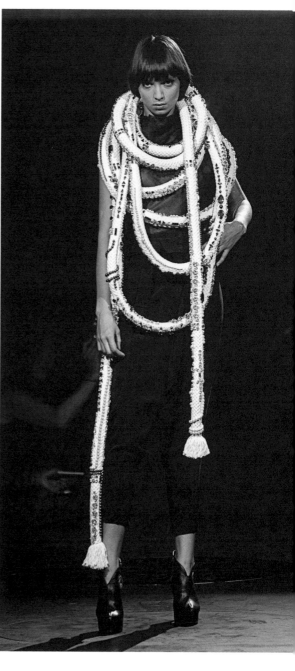

PREVIOUS PAGE, LEFT FOR AW06 LIGIA DIAS
COLLABORATED WITH COMME DES GARÇONS TO
PRODUCE A RANGE OF EMBELLISHED KNITWEAR
WHICH REFLECTED DIAS' IDIOSYNCRATIC JEWELLERY
AESTHETIC PREVIOUS PAGE, RIGHT LIGIA DIAS COLLIERS
FOR COMME DES GARÇONS AW06 ABOVE AN EMBEL-
LISHED CARDIGAN CREATED FOR COMME DES GARÇONS
AW06 RIGHT LIGIA DIAS' STRIKING CREATION FOR THE
SWAROVSKI RUNWAY ROCKS 2008 LONDON-BASED SHOW

'…some of the jewellery world's most beautiful symbols are now used with so little consideration that they are in danger of becoming devalued. The skull is a case in point. In recent years we have seen it too much in fashion jewellery, clothes, bags and even toilet paper. I don't think that customers, or even designers, know that it is part of our cultural and artistic heritage with a lot of meaning.'

OPPOSITE, TOP LEFT AND RIGHT
INSPIRED BY AN IMAGINARY LIAISON
BETWEEN DR ZHIVAGO AND TEXTILE
DESIGNER ANNI ALBERS, DIAS' AW08
COLLECTION FEATURED PEARLS
SUSPENDED IN LEATHER SWINGS,
COLOURFUL TYROLEAN RIBBONS AND
MINK POMPOMS **OPPOSITE, BELOW**
A BRACELET FROM DIAS' DEBUT AW09
MENSWEAR COLLECTION **THIS PAGE,
CLOCKWISE FROM LEFT** A NECKLACE
BY LIGIA DIAS FOR THE 3.1 PHILLIP LIM
SS08 CATWALK SHOW; A SELECTION
OF BRACELETS FROM DIAS' DEBUT
AW09 MENSWEAR COLLECTION

Marion Vidal

BEFORE EMBARKING ON HER PRESENT CAREER MARION VIDAL
STUDIED ARCHITECTURE IN PARIS AND MILAN. AS A JEWELLER
SHE APPLIES THE SAME INTELLECTUAL CONSIDERATIONS TO
DESIGNING A NECKLACE OR BROOCH AS SHE WOULD WERE SHE
PLANNING A HOUSE. THE RESULTING CERAMIC PIECES ARE
CONFIDENT EXERCISES IN SCALE, COLOUR AND HARMONY.

Marion Vidal says that if she's honest she always quite fancied a career in fashion but felt it was 'too frivolous' a subject to study so she plumped instead for a six-year architecture degree. In the event, the fashion itch persisted and so no sooner had she graduated than she enrolled at Antwerp's Royal Academy of Fine Arts where she obtained a fashion design degree in 2004.

Once embarked on her fashion career Vidal dedicated herself to designing womenswear, styling each collection with necklaces that she had also made. By the time she got to her third collection Vidal had resolved to limit herself to designing accessories – specifically bags and jewellery – in order to concentrate on a medium that afforded her greater scope to experiment with her chosen materials. She moved back to Paris and in 2006 celebrated the unveiling of her first accessories-only collection.

As luck would have it, those six years at architectural college proved not to have been entirely in vain and Vidal continues to adopt an approach to design that is still very much influenced by her early architectural training. 'For a house, you have to bear in mind that people will live inside it, for jewellery, somebody will wear it so the considerations are similar. Spatial relationships between elements and materials are important in both cases: the end result has to be comfortable and look good too. It has to give pleasure.' Ultimately, she sees the design process as a kind of juggling act. 'I play with the proportions, and then build a composition with elements and colours.'

When starting a design, Vidal sketches everywhere. On the train, at home, on every

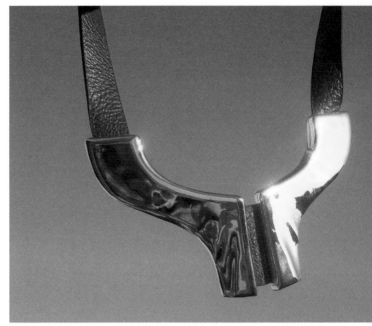

piece of paper that falls into her path.
Once a sketch is finalized she moves on to
3D-modelling that helps her resolve the balance
between individual pieces and the overall
structure. She likes the challenge of working
with materials – leather, wood and ceramic –
which are not the immediately obvious choices
for jewellery but that have potent tactile qualities.
The bonus of this approach is that she gets
to work with artisans who are brimming with
know-how and passion: 'I collaborate with
Italian, Belgian and French craftspeople who
don't usually work on jewellery. There are
ceramicists who make plates and vases and
carpenters who make furniture. It's interesting
to work with these people because their approach
to making jewellery is entirely different and so
the result is always something unique.' A case
in point is the commission she undertook for
Venetian glass company Salviati that resulted
in two collections of jewellery made with giant
blown-glass beads.

When asked how she likes her jewellery
to be worn she says that what pleases her most
is to see it appropriated and interpreted in ways
she has not considered. 'When a person gives
my pieces a new sense or uses them to create
an image that is specifically theirs, that's
something I find very satisfying.' If she's certain

of one thing, however, it's this: with their colourful
eruptions of glossy ceramic pearls, giant hand-
carved wooden beads, vibrant colours and bold
leather straps – her necklaces are most
definitely not for wallflowers.

In 2007 Vidal was commissioned to design
a collection of seven ceramic lucky charms for
Parisian fashion house, Céline. The opportunity
to work with a large design team was a first for
Vidal and an experience that she says taught her
a lot about the design process. She believes also
that such ventures are essential for designer
fashion jewellery – and the people who make
it – to thrive. 'Collaborative ventures such as
these create a real place in fashion for this niche
kind of jewellery, and that's a very positive thing.
Jewellery becomes part of the silhouette, part
of the clothes and part of the overall impression.'

Despite her enduring love affair with fashion,
however, Vidal claims to be unconcerned with
keeping her finger on the pulse of seasonal
trends. 'I do what I feel, and I have confidence
in what I want to design,' she affirms, sounding
very much like a woman who has finally found
her groove. 'To me it's more important to enjoy
what I do and to channel that philosophy into
my work so that others can derive as much
pleasure from it as I do.'
WWW.MARIONVIDAL.COM

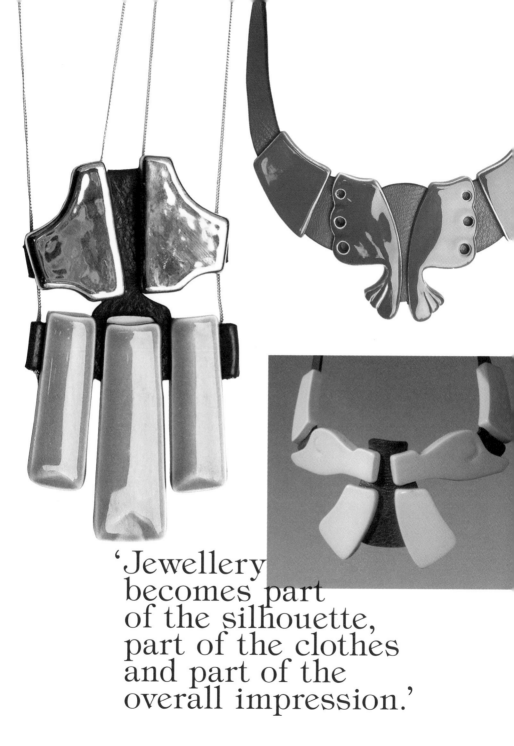

'Jewellery
becomes part
of the silhouette,
part of the clothes
and part of the
overall impression.'

OPPOSITE, BOTTOM AND TOP LEFT HAND-CARVED
WOODEN BANGLES AND CERAMIC BEAD NECKLACE –
ALL SS08 **OPPOSITE, TOP RIGHT** CERAMIC 'FOX' BROOCH
AW06 AND 'TOTEM' NECKLACE SS07 **ABOVE** A CLASSIC
VIDAL NECKLACE MADE FROM SICILIAN HAND-TURNED
WOOD AND TRIPLE-FIRED CERAMIC BEADS – FROM HER
SS08 COLLECTION

Michelle Jank

AUSTRALIAN DESIGNER MICHELLE JANK HAS BIG IDEAS – LITERALLY. SHE THINKS HER LARGE-SCALE JEWELLERY PIECES (OR GARMENT TRANSFORMERS) ARE A BREATH OF FRESH AIR FOR OUTFITS IN NEED OF A LIFT AND SHE'S CERTAIN THAT HER DREAM CLIENT – THE QUEEN OF ENGLAND – WOULD LOOK GREAT WEARING A GIANT PLATINUM BEETLE.

You've said you enjoy breaking the barrier of the traditional in jewellery. What do you mean by that?
I'm interested in blurring the line between jewellery and clothing so that you don't know where one starts and the other finishes, and I like to test notions of scale, which is why I'm drawn to large-format pieces. I also love the idea of working with reflective surfaces and watching the light interact with them. When I wear my mirrored bird necklaces they send bird reflections bouncing down the streets in the sunlight and I see people smile as I walk past.

What materials do you use?
Acrylic, magnets, metal, found objects and jersey straps to make the pieces adjustable. I think that in an over-producing society a few updated accessories might discourage people from buying superfluous clothing with a discard mentality.

What are your working methods?
In my creative life I work on lots of different projects: styling, designing clothing, costume and jewellery, creative direction, painting and writing. I find one craft feeds the others. I collate my thoughts then I internalize them and work on the physical.

What inspires you?
A Man Ray image of Nancy Cunard in her over-layered jewellery inspired me when I was very young to start what has become a pretty vast bracelet collection. Nowadays, whatever mood I'm in, natural forms – birds, flowers and stones – are always a departure point. Recently I've been hand-painting flowers and using vintage fabrics from my personal collection. As a designer it's important to reflect the wider viewpoint as well as one's own feeling so this approach feels right at the moment.

PREVIOUS PAGE A MODEL SHOWCASES PIECES FROM MICHELLE JANK'S AW08 JEWELLERY COLLECTION: THE CROWN IS CALLED 'WHERE IS THE MAN WITH THE TIARA?' WHILE THE NECKLACES ARE DUBBED 'SHE WAS A DIAMOND DANCER' AND 'A BIRD FLEW INTO MY HEART' ABOVE 'A BIRD FLEW INTO MY HEART' SS04 RIGHT 'HOW DID IT GET THAT OUT OF HAND?' SS05 OPPOSITE A SELECTION OF BROOCHES AND NECKLACES FROM JANK'S SS09 COLLECTION

'Who would be my dream client? The Queen of England. I'd make her some seriously big, elaborate diamond rings and maybe a big platinum beetle too.'

With which fashion folk have you collaborated?

I made some pieces for Undercover's Paris catwalk show in aw04/05 and then in 2007 my jewellery was shown on mannequins with smashed heads at an exhibition in their Tokyo store. Jun Takahashi (the founder of Undercover) taught me a lot about the integration of art, life and work.

For Ksubi I made charm bracelets and pendants out of powder-coated metal, with cigarette butts, toy soldiers, and other disparate found bits and pieces. And the ever-inspiring Patti Wilson commissioned me to work on pieces for Italian *Vogue*. Her brief to me was 'the bigger and madder the better.' I think we share the same heart.

Do you prefer to collaborate or work alone?

Collaborations are the key to what I do. I enjoy that process so much. Recently I've been working with the Askill brothers (Dan, Jordan and Lorin) on various projects that have really helped me spread my creative wings. They are very inspiring to work with. Patricia Field is an amazing spirit too and seeing Sarah Jessica Parker in my clothes and jewellery on the posters for season three of *Sex and the City* was up there on my list of surreal moments.

Jordan Askill is also in this book. What's the story with you two?

Jordie and I studied fashion design together at college. Since then our paths have crossed on various styling projects and then the boys created a film installation that provided the backdrop to my ss08 catwalk show at Australian Fashion Week. Jordan and I have an immediate mutual understanding that requires no catch-up conversations.

Who would be your dream client?

I'd make seriously big, elaborate diamond rings for the Queen of England. I love the idea of a twist on classical jewellery for her so I'd also make pieces which, from a distance, appear quite formal but up close are not quite what you expect. So maybe some big cast gold or platinum beetle pieces that I have been dreaming about lately. She looks magical in a tiara too. One of my favourite art images is a photograph of the Queen taken by Chris Levine which inspired one of my collections.

How important is jewellery in the grand scheme of things?

For me it's a signature. I like the idea of personal iconography so I sometimes laser etch a little poem into the back of one of my pieces so that it faces the wearer's heart. I always wear a large heart locket around my neck with a ring from Jordan Askill's first collection, and a host of keys that I have found in the streets in different places that I have travelled to and lived in…India, Paris, Australia. My work is a constant cataloguing of my travels and experiences. I am married to my jewellery: I always wear at least one piece and I'm sure I'll die wearing it too.

Naomi Filmer

STRADDLING THE BOUNDARY BETWEEN FASHION AND WEARABLE ART, NAOMI FILMER'S WORK CHALLENGES CONVENTIONAL NOTIONS OF JEWELLERY. WHETHER SHE'S USING CHOCOLATE AND ICE OR MAKING GLASS BALLS BASED ON NEGATIVE SPACE, FILMER'S LIGHT TOUCH AND CEREBRAL APPROACH HAVE BEEN BEHIND SOME OF THE CATWALK'S MOST MEMORABLE SHOWPIECES.

When asked by strangers what she does for a living Naomi Filmer says she usually offers up 'jewellery artist' by way of explanation. 'Unfortunately many people's understanding of jewellery is quite conventional and as my work is moving away from what is typically understood by the term the artist reference helps.' Making jewellery that pinches, plugs, hugs and sometimes melts, Filmer's work focuses on the relationship between object and body. 'My jewellery isn't about prettifying but about shifting the idea of preciousness away from an object's material value to the experience of wearing it.'

After graduating from the Royal College of Art in 1993 with an MA in metalwork and jewellery design Filmer started making wearable objects and had every intention of going into costume design. In art jewellery, however, she found a medium that allowed her to be more experimental by pushing the boundaries of traditional ideas of body adornment. With a growing reputation in the art world, a series of catwalk collaborations with rising British fashion stars Alexander McQueen, Julien MacDonald and Hussein Chalayan garnered Filmer critical acclaim from fashion industry insiders.

Clarifying the distinction between art and fashion jewellery Filmer, who currently lives in Milan, explains that while fashion jewellery is worn as decoration, art jewellery —as a three-dimensional expression of an idea — does not demand a wearer. 'Art jewellery celebrates ideas and craftsmanship regardless of fashion trends, and does not necessarily see the body as the initial source of inspiration.' The two fields overlap, she says, in their shared reference to the human body in terms of scale and placement.

For Filmer, the body is always her first point of inspiration. After this her focus is the context in which her work is displayed

PREVIOUS PAGE SHOULDER PIECE CREATED FROM
GOLD-PLATED POLYSTYRENE AND PLASTIC FOR ANNE
VALERIE HASH'S SS09 COUTURE SHOW **THIS PAGE** AN
ORCHID WAS THE STARTING POINT FOR A SERIES OF
NECKPIECES WHICH FILMER CONCEIVED FOR ANNE
VALERIE HASH'S SS09 COUTURE SHOW **OPPOSITE** IN 2003
FILMER DESIGNED THESE 'COUTURE ACCESSORIES' –
IN WHICH SWAROVSKI CRYSTALS ARE HELD INTO THE
RUBBER BY MEANS OF SUCTION ALONE – FOR THE
SWAROVSKI RUNWAY ROCKS EVENT WHICH TOOK
PLACE IN LONDON

and the influence this has on how it is perceived. 'A static display must endure a period of time and will be scrutinized again and again,' she explains. 'A catwalk event is quite different; it's a theatrical setting where the object is worn by a live model in motion on a runway, with music, lights, clothes, make-up, an exclusive audience and a bank of photographers. The display – which lasts mere seconds – becomes part of a bigger story.'

Beyond the catwalk, she goes on to say, the fashion world also offers the opportunity to shoot jewellery for glossy publications. 'Each stylist who works with a piece of jewellery has a different perception of the work, thereby giving it a new life. Its context can be reinvented each time which is something that doesn't happen in a gallery or museum.'

When it comes to collaborating on catwalk projects Filmer says the process always starts with a conversation between her and the designer. After this she draws and makes models to see the work in the context of the body before the final piece

is made. When Alexander McQueen asked her to design pieces for his Spanish-flavoured ss02 catwalk show Filmer visited a flamenco dancer and, watching her dance, sketched the negative space between the dancer's arm and torso as she moved. These shapes were eventually translated into a collection of hand-blown glass balls into which models inserted their hands. For French designer Ann Valerie Hash's ss09 couture show Filmer's starting point was an orchid pinned to a Barbie doll, which was developed to become a series of neckpieces created from flocked, gold-plated polystyrene and plastic.

On the challenges of creating jewellery specifically for fashion Filmer says that as an ideas person commercial viability doesn't come easily to her. She is lucky, she adds, that her senior research fellowship at Central St Martins in London enables her to pursue ideas that are initially not commercially viable, but which can be developed into marketable products.

As Filmer's work is rooted in the traditions of conceptual art, it is impossible to pigeonhole her within fashion jewellery as part of a wider trend. Even the artist herself finds it difficult to pin down her work. Her exhibitions at the Judith Clark Costume Gallery, the Mode Museum in Antwerp and London's V&A have blurred the boundaries between art, commerce and fashion, and Filmer will not limit herself to a one-dimensional description: 'I would refer to the pieces I create for the catwalk as couture accessories, or simply jewellery. My work for exhibition touches on fashion only in that it always makes a reference to body image, but otherwise I would not describe it as fashion.'

She goes on to say that while she is curious about how the body's silhouette changes according to trend she does not really follow fashion per se. 'I'm more interested in creating items that are fun, thought-provoking and that remind us of ourselves. To me, jewellery is an extension of our identity; an expression – a definition.' WWW.NAOMIFILMER.CO.UK

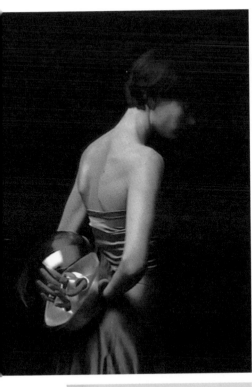

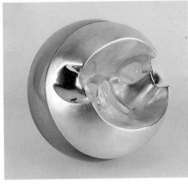

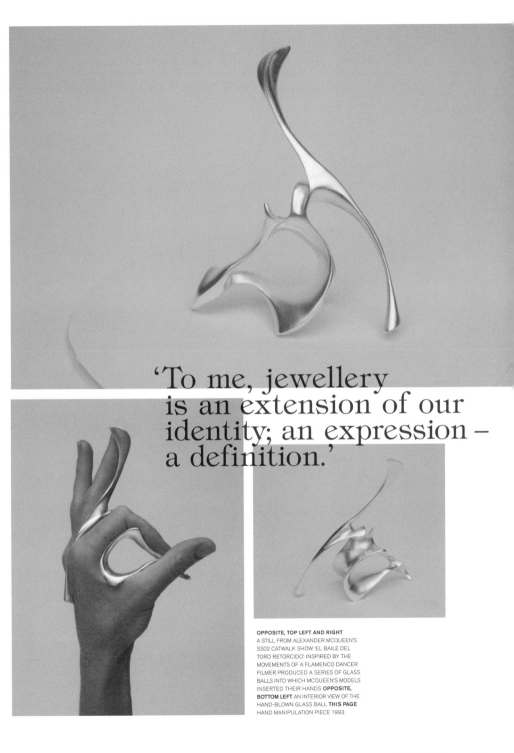

'To me, jewellery is an extension of our identity; an expression – a definition.'

Natalia Brilli

WITH HER THING FOR WRAPPING OBJECTS IN LEATHER NATALIA
BRILLI'S JEWELLERY WAS ALWAYS GOING TO BE INTERESTING.
ENCASING ITEMS SUCH AS WHISTLES, SEA URCHINS, SCARABS
AND WATCHES IN LAMBSKIN AND SUEDE SHE CREATES ONE-
OFF PIECES THAT ARE REGARDED VARIOUSLY AS FETISHISTIC
COLLECTIBLES, FASHION ACCESSORIES OR QUIRKY CURIOS.

Faced with Natalia Brilli's jewellery it comes as no surprise to learn that she hails from Belgium – a country that specializes in producing designers whose tastes err on the dark side: 'Surrealism; the ghostly atmosphere and colours of certain Northern cities; a certain absurd and nonsensical sense of humour – those are definitely recurrent elements in my work.' Further mention of her esoteric influences – the surrealistic movies of Emeric Pressburger, Jacques Tourneur's film noir and Dario Argento's horror flicks; designers Martin Margiela and Elsa Schiaparelli; decorative arts luminaries Janine Janet and Tony Duquette and songs by Nick Cave – only serve to underscore her interest in the somewhat twisted.

Before turning to fashion Brilli trained at La Cambre school in Brussels where she gained a background in theatre scenography and costume after which a move to Paris in 2003 and further studies at fashion college focused her attentions on the field of accessory design. The following year was a big one for Brilli. In addition to launching her eponymous label she joined Rochas as the luxury brand's head accessories designer in charge of producing jewellery, leather goods and eyewear. After leaving Rochas in 2006 Brilli went on to work with Loewe and AF Vandevorst – in both cases on jewellery and with the latter on bags too.

The effect Brilli's multidisciplinary education and subsequent training had was to instill in her a fascination with the applied arts as well as a strong grounding in fashion history – p articularly of the period between the World Wars. 'Those years were so rich in terms of accessories and artisanal know-how,' explains Brilli. 'I found out that covering objects in leather was a common technique in the 30s and 40s but it had subsequently fallen out of favour. I worked relentlessly, by trial and error, until I found

...the traditionally ladylike pearl necklace assumes a kinky alter-ego when wrapped in black leather...

a way to reproduce it.' The time-consuming process – everything is done entirely by hand since no machine can execute the fiddly steps – means that some of Brilli's more complex pieces can take up to two days to complete. 'When I conceive a piece of jewellery I don't attempt to reproduce reality. I'm drawn to the idea of mimesis and presenting familiar objects in unfamiliar ways. I appropriate the emblematic codes of classic jewellery but by covering objects in leather in order to leave only an imprint they become more graphic and their essence is rid of anything superfluous.' The effect is simultaneously eerie, sexy and perplexing.

But if there's something undeniably unsettling about her work there's a humour too. Devoid of detail Brilli's pieces become a sort of visual joke: the traditionally ladylike pearl necklace assumes a kinky alter-ego when wrapped in black leather; cameos have their faces obscured; scarab beetles and sea urchins are reduced to shadows dangling from sautoirs or suspended as pendants. For men too there are Rolex watches (re-named Nolexes) that will never tell the time and whistles that are eternally silent. Tightly sheathed in lambskin leather – according to Brilli 'a living, noble and sensual material that allows for incredible technical possibilities' – suede, and on occasion exotic python, pieces are coloured using a limited, but bold, palette or given distressed metallic finishes.

These days Brilli's work is stocked in over 30 countries worldwide. She puts her appeal down to a fanbase with broad-ranging tastes: 'Some people buy my jewellery to wear it as simple fashion accessories, others like to collect it as fetish pieces that they exhibit on a piece of furniture or in a glass case but whether it be fashion jewellery or collector's object, there are no set boundaries in my work. At the end of the day, each person is free to understand my work however they wish'.

For herself, Brilli says every collection takes the form of a story, a myth or an epic tale with each piece assuming an aesthetic but also symbolic dimension. 'A strong piece of fashion jewellery can embody a "couture spirit" when it's made out of rare materials, and with their limited-edition approach they acquire an exceptional character; one can buy a beautiful object that can be worn as well as displayed at home.'

'And after all,' she adds as a wry afterthought, 'it's only accessories and sometimes it's healthy not to take oneself too seriously...'

WWW.NATALIABRILLI.FR

PREVIOUS PAGE THIS MOODY SHOT
CAPTURES THE ETHEREAL NATURE
OF NATALIA BRILLI'S LEATHER-ENCASED
JEWELLERY. THESE PAGES, CLOCKWISE
FROM BOTTOM RIGHT BONE CUFFS
AW07; SEA URCHIN NECKLACE AW07;
PEARL NECKLACE AW08; A MEMENTO
MORI-INSPIRED SAUTOIR; SCARAB
BEETLE SAUTOIR AW07; WHISTLE
NECKLACE AW07; LEATHER-FEATHER
BROOCH AND NECKLACES BY NATALIA
BRILLI FOR AF VANDEVORST

The effect is simultaneously eerie, sexy and perplexing.

USING A TECHNIQUE POPULAR IN THE 1930S NATALIA BRILLI SPECIALIZES IN PRODUCING JEWELLERY AND ACCESSORIES THAT LOOK AS THOUGH THEY HAVE BEEN DIPPED IN LEATHER. **THESE PAGES, CLOCKWISE FROM BOTTOM LEFT** BRILLI'S STARK AESTHETIC ENSURES THAT HER WORK APPEALS TO MEN AND WOMEN ALIKE. HERE A MODEL WEARS A BONE NECKLACE AND LEATHER SCARF; GEMSTONE BANGLES; GEM NECKLACE AW07; SEA URCHIN SAUTOIR; NATALIA BRILLI'S NOVEL TAKE ON THE PEARL NECKLACE SEES HER COVER BEADS IN FINE WHITE LAMBSKIN LEATHER; SCARAB BEETLE CHOKER AW07; BEADED BRACELETS SS06

Philip Crangi

AS A SELF-CONFESSED AVID MATERIALIST AND AVOWED COLLECTOR PHILIP CRANGI STARTED
MAKING JEWELLERY OUT OF 'A DESIRE TO ADD TO THE FLOTSAM AROUND ME BY CREATING TONNES
OF STUFF MYSELF.' COMBINING MATERIALS NOT OFTEN ASSOCIATED WITH TRADITIONAL JEWELLERY
DESIGN HE PRODUCES WHAT HE CALLS 'HEIRLOOM PIECES AND CLASSICS FOR A NEW ERA.'

Philip Crangi is drawn to excess. 'I love textiles, embroideries, tapestries and the minute detail that goes into an overall piece. I also have a great love for the useless jewelled object: Fabergé bibelots, ornate floral arrangements and chandeliers.' This is why, he suggests, his own jewellery is so intensely detailed. 'At first glance my work appears quite simple but look closely and you'll discover many layers to it and see that it's just as intricate inside as out.'

Crangi finds inspiration everywhere, claiming that to focus on just one thing is to be unnecessarily limited. From historical references (Greco-Roman artefacts, baroque ironwork and Japanese armour) to needlepoint, maps and taxidermy he describes his aesthetic as one of contrasts in material, colour and mood.

After training as a goldsmith at the prestigious Rhode Island School of Design Crangi set up a New York-based studio from where, in 2001, he launched his first jewellery collection. Drawn to the visual tensions created by the fusion of old and new he combines classic goldsmithing methods such as engraving, with industrial techniques like laser-cutting. Gold and wrought iron often feature together in the same piece and it is not unusual for him to create a patina on stainless steel to make it look like leather. In this respect Crangi regards himself as something of an alchemist. 'I'm making the industrial transcend the source material,' he says; 'Turning something base into something of value.' Crangi makes his own models and prototypes and each piece of jewellery is produced in his New York City studio by a team of three goldsmiths who construct each individual piece by hand.

'Jewellery functions in three ways: as a memento, a talisman and a status symbol so I try to reflect those things in my work,' explains Crangi. Certainly, the multifaceted nature of his elegant designs ensure that they appeal to a broad spectrum of jewellery-lovers. New York hipsters appreciate the off-beat detailing while ladies who lunch are drawn to the novel spin he puts on traditional pieces. Men in particular buy into his work. 'For them it's less about attracting attention, more "does it look like I've had this forever?" It's like an old band T-shirt: even if you actually just spent $500 on it, it has to exude

nonchalance – as if you've treasured it since junior high.'

It was Crangi's idiosyncratic approach to fine jewellery that first led him to the fashion arena – a playground he had resisted for some time. 'I never set out to be in fashion because for me jewellery exists in a different time frame and was not always served well by something that's constantly changing.' He is the first to admit, however, that things have evolved; that fashion and jewellery have become more closely linked and that by shifting his focus he has reached a broader audience.

'For a long time jewellery played second fiddle to clothes in the fashion

industry, particularly as it moved to a more minimal look in the 90s. But over the last ten years or so I can't imagine opening a magazine and not seeing pages of editorial dripping with jewellery,' says Crangi. He puts what he calls this 'new golden age of jewellery' down to talented people who previously worked as stylists and in editorial moving into designing fashion jewellery, a medium that afforded them an opportunity because it has minimal skill-set requirements beyond a good idea and access to a technician. 'That freedom allowed a lot of people to move into this field,' says Crangi. 'It changed the discourse.'

'For men jewellery is like an old band T-shirt. Even if you've just spent a fortune on it it has to exude nonchalance – as if you've treasured it since junior high.'

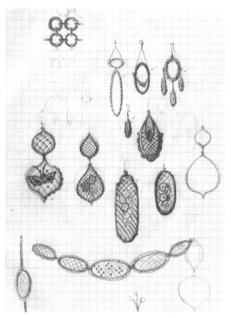

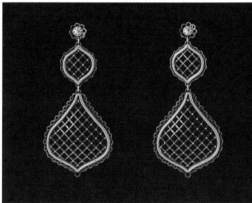

PREVIOUS PAGE FOR VERA WANG'S AW08 CATWALK SHOW CRANGI CREATED A COLLECTION OF SUPERSIZED RHINESTONE JEWELLERY THAT INCLUDED NECKLACES, RINGS AND CUFFS OPPOSITE, LEFT THIS STAINLESS STEEL AND GOLD 'BIRD OF PREY' NECKLACE IS ONE OF CRANGI'S MOST POPULAR MODELS OPPOSITE, RIGHT A CUFF FOR THE VERA WANG AW08 SHOW LEFT CRANGI'S METICULOUSLY DRAWN SKETCHES DEMONSTRATE HIS MINUTE ATTENTION TO DETAIL ABOVE 'GRENADA ARABESQUE' EARRINGS FIRST INTRODUCED IN 2007

One man's competition is another man's spur to greater things and of the rise in competition Crangi is nothing but positive. 'I love that the field has opened up and I relish those instances when I think, "I wish I'd made that." When I see something wonderful, and I feel devastated, it propels me to make better things. My favourite emotion is jealousy.'

Confirmation of his acceptance into the fashion fold came in 2007 when he won the CFDA/Vogue fashion award for best designer. Shortly thereafter he came to the attention of fashion designer Vera Wang. Spotting a piece Crangi had made for a friend she commissioned a series of leather and brass belts and bracelets for her ss08 catwalk collection. For Wang's aw08 show Crangi went back to researching and modifying old costume jewellery techniques in order to produce a collection of oversized rhinestone jewellery. Having sourced dead stock settings and antique rhinestones he looked to original costume pieces and quadrupled the scale on them sending out necklaces as thick as ropes festooned with gobstopper-sized orbs and vintage-style cocktail rings. They went into production only slightly scaled down and sold in Wang's first ready-to-wear store, which opened that autumn in New York.

When asked to elaborate on his reasons for making such an in-your-face jewellery statement Crangi explains: 'The general DNA of American fashion is much more sportswear orientated and only very recently have we started looking at ways of playing with scale. Jewellery is used very differently on our runways since both Vera and I share an interest in creating an impact in that specific moment. I wanted those pieces to come down the catwalk and challenge the audience.' More prosaically Wang reportedly referred to the fruits of their labour as jewellery 'on steroids'.

WWW.PHILIPCRANGI.COM

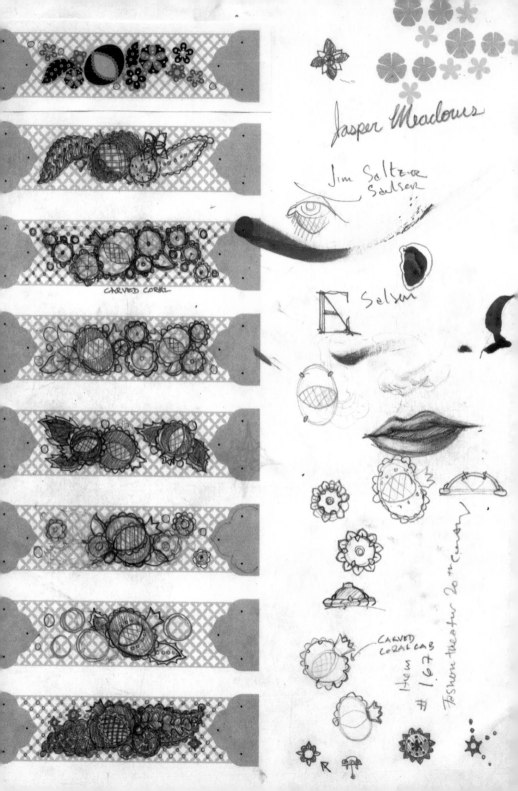

CARVED CORAL

Jasper Meadows

Jim Salter
Salser

Selser

CARVED
CORAL CAB

Item
167

Fashion theater 20 th century

'When I see something wonderful made by someone else and I feel devastated, it propels me to make better things. My favourite emotion is jealousy.'

R

AS THE BARELY-THERE NAME OF HIS COMPANY SUGGESTS
LAURENT RIVAUD IS NOT A MAN GIVEN TO BOLD STATEMENTS OR
LIMELIGHT-HOGGING. MUCH LIKE HIS ROMANTICALLY-INSPIRED
JEWELLERY – WHOSE MINUTELY DETAILED WORK IS BEST
APPRECIATED UP CLOSE AND PERSONAL – RIVAUD PREFERS
TO MAINTAIN AN AIR OF MYSTERY.

Laurent Rivaud's ascent through the ranks of fashion is the stuff of legend. While still at school the precociously talented Frenchman completed a work experience placement in the atelier of the legendary Thierry Mugler. 'It was so grand in the late 80s,' he recalls. 'They set me to work with the fashion and accessories teams and since there were no limits on our budget we were sending things down the catwalks that had never been witnessed before. Back then Mugler was amazing; so poetic.'

In 1989, shortly after graduating from Paris' Studio Berçot, the fledgling fashion designer scored his first jewellery job – and second major fashion coup – working for none other than Yves Saint Laurent. His commission was to produce a jewellery collection for one of Saint Laurent's haute couture shows. 'It was incredible. In the offices there were Warhol's on the walls and although I'd never made jewellery before I compensated by being young and full of confidence. I just assured them

I could do it!' Using crocodile skin, giant semi-precious stones and a big and bold aesthetic he produced a collection whose 'rough feel' was an acclaimed hit. It was also his access-all-areas golden ticket into fashion's rarefied echelons: 'That experience was the best possible CV. From there I went on to Givenchy while Monsieur Givenchy was still at the helm and after that to Chloé.'

When Vivienne Westwood wanted to launch a jewellery line it was to Rivaud that she turned. The year was 1994 and to this day Rivaud's hand is behind each collection. But while the birds, devil-horn headbands and glittering orbs that have become iconic Westwood jewels may have had their genesis in Rivaud's imagination, he is quick to renounce all ownership and deflects further questioning, saying only that 'it is all Vivienne's'.

He's scarcely more readily drawn on his own label, R, which he founded in 2003, as a platform to realize his unadulterated

vision of jewellery. What he will say is that he is most keen on the research aspect of his work that leads him to spend inordinate amounts of time immersed in books or visiting museums and galleries. 'I view each new collection as an excuse to learn so many things. I spend ages on the research process – too long; I get carried away!' Successive collections have seen him turn for reference to the spread of Japonisme through Europe, old legends of the Rhine, Victorian phantasmagoria, 1930s decadence and the life and times of Fortunato Pio Castellani – a nineteenth-century Italian who found fame reproducing the jewellery designs he unearthed on archaeological digs and a man whose ethos chimes with Rivaud's.

When it comes to synthesizing his ideas, Rivaud begins to draw. Once a design is perfected it is translated into a 3D version by a team of model-makers and Rivaud then travels to Thailand where the final pieces are made up, using classic goldsmithing techniques. At this point Rivaud dons his learning hat once more: 'I'm not hands-on at the making stage but I'm very interested in the techniques. I really love spending time with the craftspeople and watching the skill with which they work.'

A piece of R jewellery is instantly recognizable from its antique appearance, an effect that is achieved through Rivaud's use of traditional jewellery design details and the inclusion of whimsical

figurative elements such as monkeys, bird skulls and grinning masks. Contrary to received wisdom about pairing gold and silver Rivaud combines the two materials and much-used signature details include glinting pave marcasite, multi-stranded chains, malachite plugs, oxidized silver tassels, antique coins, griffon's claws clasping pearls and graduated beads made from semi-precious stones.

That Rivaud chooses to express himself in this aesthetic is strange because, while his work is very much grounded in the tradition of heirlooms and talismans, he is by his own admission not an overly sentimental man. Asked what he would save in the event of a fire his answer is an unequivocal, if brief: 'just one ring.'

Unsurprisingly, he finds inspiration in somewhat melancholy places: nineteenth-century mourning jewellery and memento mori, Arthur Rackham's illustrations, Victorian paintings of Alma Tadema and Lord Leighton, and music by PJ Harvey. But despite the gloomy references Rivaud doesn't appreciate the all-too-obvious labels people apply to his work. 'It's often referred to as gothic but that's not it at all. Dark is where I'm at and what's more there's a humour to it.' By way of proof he points to his first sweet-inspired Candy collection that featured realistic, shiny-wrapped bon bons, and to his latest collection, which has a family of colourful bugs as its central cast of characters. 'You see,' he says, 'I have fun with it too.'

PREVIOUS PAGE CLOSE-UP DETAIL
OF THE AW08 'NARCISSUS' NECKLACE
SHOWING SEVERAL R SIGNATURES: PAVE
MARCASITE, HEAVY SILVER LINKS, THE R
INITIAL INCLUDED ON EVERY PIECE AND
A SECTION OF HAND-CARVED ONYX TO
EMBELLISH THE FASTENING **OPPOSITE,
LEFT** THIS 'FIDES AMOR' NECKLACE FROM
R'S SS07 COLLECTION SHOWS ANOTHER
TRADEMARK FEATURE – THE USE OF
BOTH GOLD AND SILVER IN ONE PIECE
OPPOSITE, RIGHT DETAIL FROM A TRIPLE-
STRANDED, MOTHER-OF-PEARL BEADED
NECKLACE **LEFT** ANIMAL MOTIFS ARE
A KEY FEATURE IN R COLLECTIONS AND
NONE MORE SO THAN THE BIRD HEAD
SEEN HERE SUSPENDED ON A BROOCH

...inspiration is found in somewhat melancholy places: nineteenth-century mourning jewellery and memento mori; Arthur Rackham's illustrations, Victorian paintings by Alma Tadema and Lord Leighton, and music by PJ Harvey.

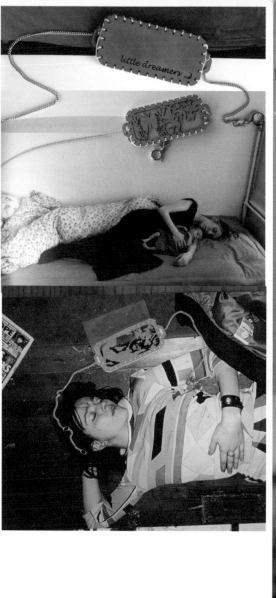

Sabrina Dehoff

GOOD THINGS COME IN SMALL PACKAGES – ESPECIALLY IN SABRINA DEHOFF'S MINIATURE WORLD. IT WAS 'AN INTEREST IN THE TINY PARTS, FINISHINGS AND EMBELLISHMENTS ON CLOTHES' THAT FIRST PROMPTED THE BERLIN-BASED FASHION DESIGNER AND CONSULTANT TO LAUNCH HER OWN JEWELLERY LINE. THAT, AND A DESIRE TO TELL HER 'LITTLE STORIES'.

In 1996, shortly after obtaining a degree in womenswear design from London's Royal College of Art, Sabrina Dehoff landed a plum role as Alber Elbaz's design assistant at Guy Laroche. Two years and a move to Lanvin later Dehoff was promoted to senior design assistant under the fashion house's then creative head Cristina Ortiz.

In 2005, buoyed by her experiences and keen to branch out on her own, Dehoff returned to her native Berlin and launched Vonrot: a fashion consultancy whose clients have to date included Moschino, DKNY and Sportmax. That same year she also founded Sabrina Dehoff Accessories and began designing her own line of jewellery.

The move into accessories was a natural one for Dehoff. 'As a womenswear designer I was known for a modern, clean look but at the same time I was constantly looking for new approaches to detailing, in particular when it came to the embellishment on each piece. I also loved to make up little stories to go with each collection so I guess it was a combination of those interests that inspired my decision to start making jewellery. It's also a really great way to experiment because you get results much more quickly.'

Dehoff called her debut collection Little Helpers and billing it as 'an exclusive remedy for various occasions' she unveiled a range of cute puffy figurines – peace doves, guitars, cowboy boots and love hearts – all handmade from fine glove leather. Other collections followed: Little Dreamers included a set of 23-carat gold fruit silhouettes; Epigenetics Vs Atomists was all about cashmere pompoms inspired by molecular structures, and Erratic Blocks from the Trip to the Moon featured a cast of tiny animals made out of acrylic and precious metal. Each collection is completely different in appearance and

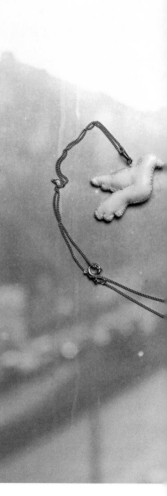

PREVIOUS PAGE SABRINA DEHOFF PUTS ALMOST AS MUCH EFFORT INTO PRODUCING HER WHIMSICAL LOOKBOOKS AS SHE DOES HER JEWELLERY. THESE IMAGES SHOW NOT ONLY PIECES FROM HER FINISHED COLLECTION BUT THE INSPIRATIONS BEHIND IT **ABOVE AND RIGHT** LOOKBOOK PAGES FEATURING MINIATURE LEATHER FIGURINES FROM DEHOFF'S DEBUT COLLECTION 'LITTLE HELPERS' AW06

mood but shares a miniature sense of scale. Dehoff's interest in making up tales and her attention to detail are reflected in the lookbooks (or more accurately, storybooks) she produces to accompany each collection. On every page collaged images are assembled from illustrations, scribbled sayings or fragments of poetry and photos superimposed with shots of her fanciful jewellery.

'I guess it's for my own personal sense of fun that I invent those stories. I just love immersing myself in these new worlds and researching into the topics that suddenly seem to be the right ones.' Depending on the scenario some pieces of jewellery play character roles, but Dehoff says that ultimately for her it's more about 'subverting the symbols of prettiness, cuteness, coolness and glamour.'

Dehoff – who makes a point of exploring a different material each season, be it wood, silk, metal or crystal – begins each collection by 'sketching, researching and tinkering about' until she hones in on an idea for the right technique and form. All metalwork elements are manufactured by specialists but anything that can be assembled by hand – sewing, pompom producing and leather cutting – are all carried out in Dehoff's studio.

Summarizing her design philosophy as 'idealistic and fatalistic,' Dehoff draws on an extensive reserve of inspirations including: 'everything and nothing, good taste, bad taste, anything ugly and everything beautiful, crown jewels, motor sections, molecular biology, ants, serious talks, silly talks, things that I adore, things that I hate, things I long for, things that intimidate me.' Being in the playground, chatting to her friends and watching her children growing, are also moments that furnish her with ideas, and no doubt, the source of the pleasure she takes in storytelling.

Asked what it is exactly that she finds so appealing about jewellery Dehoff is unable to pinpoint one particular thing. Broadly speaking, she thinks it has a lot to do with communication: 'The way we dress is mostly about styling, and jewellery is a great way to personalize a style and as well as saying something about ourselves. It enables us to create a look which is embellished and pure and modern at the same time.'

Ultimately Dehoff says her dream is to produce two jewellery lines: one dedicated to smaller, wearable pieces, the other devoted to showpieces and a couture range that she would present each season as part of a show. At the moment she is expanding into textile design and has produced a number of printed fabric pieces which – combined with metal embellishments – straddle the boundary between fashion accessory and jewellery. Dehoff says that 'exciting collaborations' are also underway although she has to keep them under her hat for now. Whatever they are, they're bound to end up happily ever after.

WWW.SABRINADEHOFF.COM

'Ultimately, for me, designing jewellery is about subverting the symbols of prettiness, cuteness, coolness and glamour.'

OPPOSITE AS SEEN FROM THE
TINY SCALE OF THESE PIECES FROM
HER 'NATURESQUE' SS09 COLLECTION
SABRINA DEHOFF HAS AN INTEREST
IN ALL THINGS MINIATURE **THIS PAGE,
CLOCKWISE FROM BOTTOM** NECKLACES
FROM THE 'ME PAIRED YOUNITED'
AW08 COLLECTION; A SEGMENTED
METAL DASCHUND FROM THE SAME
COLLECTION; IMAGES FROM THE
LOOKBOOK THAT ACCOMPANIED
DEHOFF'S 'LITTLE DREAMERS'
SS07 COLLECTION

Scott
Stephen

EXOTIC, ELABORATE AND VIBRANT – SCOTT STEPHEN'S JEWELLERY
BELIES HIS ORIGINS IN THE CHILLY SCOTTISH CITY OF DUNDEE.
HIS ONE-OF-A KIND PIECES ARE STEPHEN'S WAY OF CONJURING
UP 'EXOTIC WORLDS AND FASCINATING CHARACTERS', AND
WITH EACH HAND-CRAFTED BEAD TAKING UP TO FIVE HOURS
TO ASSEMBLE, THEY'RE ALSO A SERIOUS LABOUR OF LOVE.

In the beginning…
I graduated in 2000 with a BA in printed
textiles. From Dundee I went straight
to Milan where I found myself designing
couture fabrics for the likes of Jean Paul
Gaultier and Christian Dior. I adored
the job but little by little the limitations
in terms of how much personal input
I could offer got to me.

How did you find your direction?
I used to take home remnants, mainly
Chanel tweeds and bouclés, and I began
to make little pieces – flowers and the like.
I gave them away to friends and family and
got such a great response that I made an
appointment to see the buyers at Liberty.
They bought the first collection and
I moved down to London.

With which fashion designers have
you collaborated?
I created a range of mixed material
necklaces and earrings for Dries Van Noten
to complement his aw05 collection, which
sold exclusively in his flagship Antwerp
store. For Swarovski Runway Rocks in 2007
I designed a bejewelled multi-stranded body
piece with detachable epaulettes. The
inspiration for that piece was the imperial
Russian court, the heavily worked pelisse
of a Russian General and the splendour
of the Grand Duchess Vladimir.

How should your jewellery
to be worn?
Boldly and courageously: as a statement
of the wearer's personality. I also like
to think of my jewellery in a more
intimate setting where a woman lavishly
bejewels herself without inhibition,
as if she's playing dress-up. I often
include hats, bags, epaulettes and
headpieces in my collections so they
can be used to enhance the jewellery
by developing a theme.

What do you strive to achieve
with your work?
There's no great master plan but I do
aim to make pieces that alert the senses;
that demand to be touched or appear
almost edible at times. Jewellery is about
ornamentation – it has to be beautiful to
wear but also incredibly tactile. It should
be something you want to touch and
explore again and again.

What inspires you?
Colour is the key to every collection
I design: skin-toned pink; lapis lazuli,
peacock and sky blues; mint greens;
nuances of plum and sage; old gold, thick
treacle; bronze and jet; rich purples; vivid
magentas and deep golds. They're all
in there somewhere.

PREVIOUS PAGES SCOTT STEPHEN
METICULOUSLY ASSEMBLES EACH
ELEMENT OF HIS OFTEN ORNATE
JEWELLERY BY HAND. THESE EARRINGS
WERE CREATED BY WRAPPING BASE
BEADS OF DIFFERING SIZES IN FINE
GOLD AND SILVER CHAIN THESE PAGES,
CLOCKWISE FROM FAR LEFT A CORSAGE
FROM THE 'BIBA' SS06 COLLECTION;
NECKLACE DETAIL; AN EVOCATIVE
EDITORIAL SHOT PUTS STEPHEN'S
JEWELLERY CENTRE STAGE; 'BIBA'
CORSAGE; NO TWO BEADS ON A SCOTT
STEPHEN NECKLACE ARE ALIKE;
FRONTISPIECE TO THE 'BIBA' COLLECTION
LOOKBOOK

How do you manage to keep your work fresh?

By playing with the materials I have at hand and pushing them beyond their conventional applications. I never know where they'll take me but that's the essential part of the overall adventure.

What are the challenges of creating your jewellery?

The obvious challenge for me is that I have no jewellery-making skills in the conventional sense. I've had to draw upon my skills as a textile designer to carve my niche in the industry. Also, I hand-make every piece myself and it's not unusual for me to spend five hours perfecting a single bead. So, factor in a minimum of 20 beads for one necklace and you can see that what I do becomes a real labour of love.

Why so long?

First I layer the base beads. Then I might cover that layer in Chantilly lace or silk tulle to which I'll apply micro sequins, hematite chips and scatterings of crystal. Here and there I'll cut the lace away to reveal the beads underneath. On other occasions you might find me making beads from embroidery silks, fine leather strips and gold chains. That's why it takes so long!

Is jewellery important?

Yes, because it is worn for many different reasons. As a sentimental token or a gesture of love, death, remembrance and ceremony. It is also a vehicle for us to display a facet of our personality. Fashion jewellery in particular makes more of an impact because there are fewer limits on size, shape and materials so the outcome is far more interesting than with fine jewellery.

How would you summarize your design philosophy?

Frivolity and opulence. When I design my goal is to create jewellery that conjures up exotic worlds and fascinating characters. The idea is that each collection tells us something about a different place or era.

How has your work been described?

Depending on the collection it has been described as: the Scottish Highlands seen through the eyes of a Bohemian naturalist with a penchant for absinthe; flower petals embellished with hundreds of dewdrop-like glass beads; mad, bad and dangerous to know punk fetish; an African safari through lush jungles and desert plains; a disco hustle with Bianca and Grace in stacked platforms and plunging necklines; glitterball bibelots.

WWW.SCOTTSTEPHEN.CO.UK

'How should
my jewellery
be worn?
Boldly and
courageously:
as a statement
of the wearer's
personality.'

OPPOSITE 'KIM' (LEFT) AND 'VIVIENNE'
(RIGHT) NECKLACES FROM STEPHEN'S
'PUNK CHIC' AW07 COLLECTION **THIS
PAGE, CLOCKWISE FROM BELOW**
NECKLACE DETAIL; SCOTT STEPHEN'S
STORAGE SYSTEM; BEADS IN VARIOUS
STAGES OF COMPLETION

Scott Wilson

'SCOTT HAS A VISION THAT IS TRULY UNIQUE. HIS STAND-OUT SCULPTURAL PIECES HAVE AN EDGE OF LUXE THAT I JUST ADORE. EACH PIECE IS HIGHLY ARTISTIC AND HAND-CRAFTED YET HOLDS A STRONG MODERNITY THAT NEVER FAILS TO UP THE COOL FACTOR OF ANY OUTFIT.' YASMIN SEWELL CHIEF CREATIVE CONSULTANT, LIBERTY OF LONDON

When it comes to the catwalk Scott Wilson's penchant for designing showpieces that exist within nebulously defined boundaries is, he claims, the product of his training at London's Royal College of Art. 'Underpinning much of our studies was the notion that jewellery can, broadly speaking, be anything which relates to the body. I guess for that reason my concept of what constitutes the form is rather more flexible than other people's might be.'

After completing a degree in jewellery design at Middlesex University, an MA in womenswear and millinery from the RCA left Wilson with a fascination for creating headwear/jewellery hybrids that have become something of a signature when designing spectacular catwalk statements. Over the years these have included a series of dramatic insect-inspired headpieces for Thierry Mugler's debut couture show; undulating metallic feather helmets for Givenchy and the headgear Madonna wore to promote her album, Hard Candy.

But it is for long-time collaborator, Hussein Chalayan, that Wilson has gone all out creating – at one time or another – flocked and beaded middle eastern-style masks, architectural glass, mirror and acrylic visors and veils from cascading strands of beads. Of what he refers to as their 'rich, enjoyable and longlasting' partnership Chalayan has said: 'I see Scott as a body sculptor with a wide level of expertise, he has a real understanding of many facets of design which often fits into fashion but also extends beyond it.'

In 1997 Wilson launched his eponymous jewellery line and when not collaborating with the great and good of the fashion world it is to this that he devotes his time. He designs two distinct collections: Scott Wilson Couture – handmade jewellery that is produced as a limited number of one-season-only pieces – and a ready-to-wear range, which is a pared-down version of the couture line, available to order throughout the year.

'I think that more often than not the first idea is the best one and you don't need to fuss with that too much.'

PREVIOUS PAGE STYLIST SARAH RICHARDSON COMMISSIONED THESE ONE-OFF EARRINGS FROM SCOTT WILSON FOR A SHOOT WHICH RAN IN *iD* MAGAZINE **THIS PAGE, BACKGROUND** A SELECTION OF PIECES FROM SCOTT WILSON'S AW09 COLLECTION; A MODEL WEARS A SEQUINNED CUFF MADE BY SCOTT WILSON FOR MATTHEW WILLIAMSON'S AW07 CATWALK SHOW **OPPOSITE, LEFT** THESE DECO-INSPIRED NECKLACES BY SCOTT WILSON FOR 3.1 PHILLIP LIM AW08 FEATURED GOLD METAL ROPES PUNCTUATED WITH COLOURFUL ENAMEL DISCS **OPPOSITE, RIGHT** WILSON PRODUCED THIS HEADPIECE OF UNDULATING METALLIC FEATHERS FOR THE GIVENCHY HAUTE COUTURE CATWALK SHOW AW02

Inspired by fine art, sculpture and what he terms '70s retro-futurism' Wilson creates bright and bold jewellery from acrylic; a material about which he can wax endlessly lyrical. 'Acrylic is just so versatile: depending on whether you mould it with a heat gun or stick it in the oven, laser-cut it or machine-cut it you get very different effects. But if you want to be really specific about the outcome, shaping it by hand gives absolutely the best result.' The irony is, says Wilson, that he actually hand-finishes every piece in order to give it a slick, machined look.

Wilson works hard and fast and says that he has done so ever since his MA days when a scholarship to work in Karl Lagerfeld's Parisian atelier taught him what it was to graft: 'I was mainly working on jewellery and accessories for Karl and there was definitely no time for slacking!' He also developed a taste for uncomplicated design. 'I can't take too much decoration, my brain's simple in that respect. My style and my tastes err on the classic side.' He doesn't draw or use a computer to plan his work. 'In truth I'm pretty low tech – I think that more often than not the first idea is the best one and you don't need to fuss with that too much.' With the exception of pieces that require electroforming (which are sent away to be done) most of his considerable body of work is produced in a small east London studio where he works with just a couple of assistants.

Asked what aspect of his work gives him the greatest pleasure Wilson says it is creating one-off pieces – what he refers to as 'the ultimate expression of my work'. On a day-to-day basis he relishes the challenge of turning his ideas into reality. 'I'm not intellectual but I think my ideas can be. So while they're not conceptual they're multi-levelled in terms of problem solving. Working through things and finding a solution is definitely my strength. I also love how someone else's input can alter the direction of a project or idea.'

That he likes to collaborate is clear from his CV which boasts two full pages of high-profile fashion projects. He has produced catwalk jewellery for shows including, but not limited to, Jean Paul Gaultier couture, Valentino and Burberry menswear, and the womenswear shows of Rifat Ozbek, Julien MacDonald, 3:1 Phillip Lim and Matthew Williamson. The last of these collections comprised a series of spherical, sequined cuffs that had fashion editors the length and breadth of the industry clamouring to feature them in their magazines. Wilson is the man stylists such as Jane How, Patti Wilson and Sarah Richardson go to when they want bespoke jewellery pieces for their fashion shoots: re-working day-to-day objects into pieces of 'bricolage art.' Wilson has been known to turn afro-combs and buttons into necklaces and bones into earrings.

In light of this impressive client list it comes as something of a surprise to learn that Wilson still harbours an as yet unfulfilled ambition: to work with Balenciaga and Lanvin. If past performance is anything to go by it won't be long before he's adding a third page to that CV.

WWW.SCOTTWILSONLONDON.COM

...re-working day-to-day objects into pieces of 'bricolage art' Wilson has been known to turn afro-combs and buttons into necklaces and bones into earrings.

THESE PAGES, CLOCKWISE FROM ABOVE SHOTS OF SCOTT WILSON'S WORKBENCH AT HIS STUDIO IN EAST LONDON; LIGHTNING-STYLE EARRINGS FROM WILSON'S AW09 COLLECTION; A MODEL SPORTS A SCULPTURAL CUFF DESIGNED BY WILSON FOR PETER PILOTTO'S AW09 CATWALK SHOW; THIS BEADED HEADPIECE WAS CREATED TO ACCOMPANY HUSSEIN CHALAYAN'S 'SCENT OF THE TEMPESTS' SHOW AW97; FLORAL DESIGNS CREATED FROM SEMI-PRECIOUS STONES FEATURED IN THE SCOTT WILSON COUTURE COLLECTION AW08

Shaoo

WITH A LOVE OF FLEA MARKETS, ANTIQUE LACE AND ANCIENT CHINESE CULTURE WENWEI TONG DESCRIBES HERSELF AS AN OLD-FASHIONED GIRL WHO LIKES TO FILTER THOSE PASSIONS INTO HER JEWELLERY. BUT THERE'S MORE TO IT THAN THAT. FROM BREASTBONE-FANNING LEATHER COLLARS TO CARVED JADE ROSETTES, TONG'S TRINKETS MAY REFLECT HER OLD-SCHOOL INTERESTS BUT A LIBERAL DASH OF ROCK-CHICK ATTITUDE KEEPS THEM JUST THE WRONG SIDE OF 'NICE'.

Wenwei Tong studied fine art in Shanghai for no fewer than eight years before she moved to Paris in pursuit of a career as a womenswear designer. In 2006, after completing an internship with John Galliano, she had a change of heart and launched her jewellery label, Shaoo.

Given her upbringing it was probably inevitable that Tong's cultural interests would eventually inform her work. The name Shaoo is itself a play on words that alludes to her Chinese heritage: 'My father is a very famous calligrapher and antiquities expert so he has a sensitivity for words that carry great meaning. He's also really good at picking names so when I founded my company I asked him to help me to choose one that was strong and enigmatic.' Broadly speaking the word shao implies 'imaginary music that is both royal and mysterious'. She added the second 'o' because she liked the way it looked.

For her love of all things feminine Tong has another family member to thank. As a movie star in 30s Shanghai, her grandmother amassed a collection of clothes that was to make a lasting impression on the young Wenwei. 'I remember playing dress-up and rummaging through wardrobes packed with vintage furs and lace – it was always such an adventure.' When she began to make jewellery Tong says: 'I wanted to figure out a way to make pieces that would go with those clothes which is why nowadays what I make is an interpretation of classic jewellery with a fashionable twist.' Indeed, despite the old-school references, Tong says that contemporary fashion is always her prime motivator. 'Living in Paris I see all the trends on the catwalks and I channel those into my work. In a similar spirit I make sure that, while they have certain

'It's important to me that my jewellery is not too "nice": it's old-style but rock.'

themes in common, each collection takes a different direction to those that have gone before.'

To begin with Tong designed a collection of simple calf-leather necklaces constructed using ancient paper-cutting techniques. Inspired by antique lace the resulting pieces either spread across the breastbone like an ornate bib or scrolled close around the neck. As her collections developed over subsequent seasons Tong moved to a more cartoon-like aesthetic with oversized diamond silhouettes and metallic finishes that gently lampooned the bling culture prevalent at the time. As an added extra, each piece was reversible, with a different colour on each side.

Five sell-out collections down the line Tong felt she'd reached the limits of what she could do with leather and, wanting to express herself in a more luxurious manner, she began the hunt for a new material. Researching the jewellery of China's ancient kings she surprised herself by opting for jade – a stone she always found to be extremely ugly: 'In my mind it was associated with the Buddhas that tourists buy – I'd certainly never connected it with fashion.' What she discovered made her realize she'd found the perfect material with which to embody her ideas. As China's imperial gem, jade had for hundreds of years been more valuable than gold and silver. It embodied the Confucian virtues of wisdom, justice, compassion, modesty and courage and, most pertinently, it symbolized the female-erotic. Problem solved, Tong resolved to find a way to produce jewellery that would showcase Chinese arts and skills (all her pieces are hand-crafted by Shanghai-based artisans) while designing a collection that would appeal to a contemporary audience.

Her first piece, an ornately carved slab of white jade set on a simple gold mount, was based on a centuries-old lace panel that had once belonged to a Chinese queen. The rest of the collection included rings sporting black jade roses set on lace-inspired gold bands, carved jade button earrings and fanciful Italianate pendants dripping with pearls to resemble 'the kind of thing a woman might wear in a Botticelli painting.'

Despite the move to a more luxurious means of expression, smaller production volumes and a new market, Tong says her basic approach hasn't changed that much. Her work is still concerned with putting a modern slant on the age-old female desire to look beautiful. 'Nowadays men and women have similar roles in the world and women are able to express their strong character. But while we are no longer like dolls we are feminine and we want things to be both pretty and have personality. For that reason it's important to me that my jewellery is not too "nice": it's old-style but rock.'

WWW.SHAOO.FR

...a cartoon-like aesthetic of oversized diamond silhouettes and metallic finishes lampooned bling culture.

PAGE 166 HAND-CARVED JADE AND
PEARLS FORM THE BASIS OF SHAOO'S AW08
COLLECTION **PREVIOUS PAGE** A SELECTION
OF RINGS AND NECKLACES FROM SHAOO'S
AW08 COLLECTION WHICH WAS INSPIRED
BY ANTIQUE LACE AND ANCIENT CHINESE
CULTURE **OPPOSITE** THE INTRICATE NATURE
OF THESE NECKLACES FROM SHAOO'S SS07
COLLECTION WAS ACHIEVED BY APPLYING
ANCIENT PAPER-CUTTING TECHNIQUES TO
LEATHER **ABOVE** A DISPLAY OF THE SS07
COLLECTION AT PARISIAN BOUTIQUE COLETTE

Sonia Boyajian

SPONTANEOUS, COLOURFUL AND A TOUCH ECCENTRIC – IT COULD BE SAID THAT SONIA BOYAJIAN IS THE LIVING EMBODIMENT OF HER JEWELLERY. ASSEMBLING THE TRINKETS, BAUBLES AND PLASTIC FISH SHE AMASSES ON HER MANY ROUND-THE-WORLD ADVENTURES BOYAJIAN BUILDS COLLECTIONS THAT BREAK THE RULES.

Sonia Boyajian reckons a love of fashion is encoded in her genes. As a child her favourite pastime was to watch her mother get dressed-up before a night out, and to this day her grandmother remains a sartorial inspiration: 'She always wears high heels, vivid colours and a lot of finery. When I was little we'd find broken jewellery at the flea markets and she'd show me how to fix it.'

In 2001 fashion graduate Boyajian – an American of Armenian descent – moved to Antwerp on a whim because, 'I thought that a Belgium fashion house would be a good first step on the ladder.' An accidental meeting in the street with local jeweller Pascal Masselis led to an apprenticeship during which Boyajian learned to work with precious metals

and stones. In one weekend 20 of her pieces were sold straight from the display window. Her aptitude was such that when fashion designer Bernhard Willhem needed jewellery for his fashion shows in Paris he came knocking on Sonia's door. 'Being a very whimsical designer Bernhard had me do peculiar little projects for his runway. One time he sent me into the woods to collect sticks and he told me to make a skirt out of them. He always encouraged me to use the most unexpected materials to create things.' It was an early lesson in eclecticism that fired Boyajian's imagination.

The following year Boyajian returned to Los Angeles and, inspired by her European successes, she launched a jewellery line from her Hollywood-based

studio – a space that is by all accounts a reflection of her Bohemian tastes and filled with flowers, furniture made by friends, paper birds and trees dripping with baubles.

Boyajian's jewellery functions along similar lines – flirtatious, experimental and off-kilter it is packed with bursts of colour, clashes of texture and combinations of materials that shouldn't work together but do. Using sterling silver and gold-fill metal wire to construct her own chains or to encase crystals and semi-precious stones her pieces have a charmingly homemade appeal that shouldn't, however, be mistaken for a lack of seriousness about her work. Boyajian is, after all, the jeweller to whom Scarlett Johansson turned when she needed someone to design her infamous three-carat diamond engagement ring.

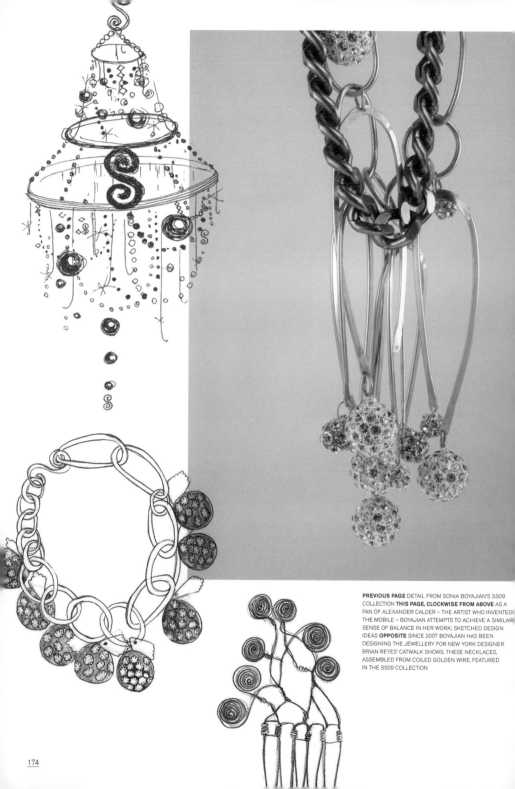

PREVIOUS PAGE DETAIL FROM SONIA BOYAJIAN'S SS09 COLLECTION THIS PAGE, CLOCKWISE FROM ABOVE AS A FAN OF ALEXANDER CALDER – THE ARTIST WHO INVENTED THE MOBILE – BOYAJIAN ATTEMPTS TO ACHIEVE A SIMILAR SENSE OF BALANCE IN HER WORK; SKETCHED DESIGN IDEAS OPPOSITE SINCE 2007 BOYAJIAN HAS BEEN DESIGNING THE JEWELLERY FOR NEW YORK DESIGNER BRIAN REYES' CATWALK SHOWS. THESE NECKLACES, ASSEMBLED FROM COILED GOLDEN WIRE, FEATURED IN THE SS09 COLLECTION

As an inveterate globetrotter – Boyajian's travels have seen her pass through Finland, Hong Kong, Thailand, Bali, Egypt, Belgium, Japan, France, Syria, Africa and Venezuela to name a few – her adventures furnish her with the materials she incorporates into her jewellery: plastic animals, hand-soldered flowers, antique watches, precious stones, imitation pearls, wooden trinkets and globules moulded from resin and hand-blown glass. The journeys themselves are a source of inspiration too: 'I saw how those cultures use their crafts and live with them on a daily basis and I wanted to reflect that in my jewellery.'

When it comes to assembling her trinkets Boyajian likes to work alone. 'I spread all my baubles and beads in front of me and slowly patchwork them together. I enjoy mixing different media in the same colours together to see what appears: there's something really satisfying about seeing a gold-coloured rhinestone with a gold-plated bead and a golden pearl all jumbled together.'

In addition to her colour experiments Boyajian endeavours to include an animal motif in each collection. 'Mostly there are always birds but Bambi has put in an appearance too and I made some lovely pieces with little wooden animal beads I bought in Africa.' Another collection featured fish and crystal beads because, 'I suppose at the time I was feeling a bit like I was swimming in two different directions at once and fish swim in clear water which is what crystal looks like to me.'

A preoccupation with equilibrium and light informs her work and as a fan of Alexander Calder – the artist who invented the mobile – she says: 'There is a certain balance to his work that I tried to emulate in mine. I suppose I try to create my own mobiles with jewellery. I was also very inspired by the way chandeliers drape so I try to make necklaces that look like chandeliers for the neck.'

In 2007 Boyajian embarked on a collaborative venture with New York designer Brian Reyes for whose catwalk shows she has been making jewellery ever since. 'It's an easygoing relationship in which Brian talks me through his inspirations and I just go with them from there.' Successive seasons have seen Boyajian create coiled gold wire cones, semi-precious stone cluster necklaces and floriform brooches.

And with her eccentric reputation preceding her it was only natural that when Comme des Garçons came to town with their LA pop-up store in 2008 she was invited to showcase a selection of her work. Threading jewellery through an industrial metal frame that was overgrown with shrubbery the coral beads, wooden discs and clear plastic fish that festooned her necklaces burst through the foliage like bizarre ripe fruit. Asked at the time why she opted for such an unconventional display she said simply, 'I like to break the rules.'

WWW.SONIABSTYLE.COM

THIS PAGE MUCH OF BOYAJIAN'S QUIRKY JEWELLERY, SUCH AS THESE NECKLACES FROM HER SS09 COLLECTION, ARE ASSEMBLED FROM FOUND OBJECTS AND FEATURE ANIMALS AND BIRDS OPPOSITE CLOSE-UP DETAILS OF A NECKLACE FROM BOYAJIAN'S SS09 COLLECTION; 'LITTLE SEÑORITA' SKETCH

...her globetrotting adventures furnish her with the materials she incorporates into her jewellery.

Sonja Bischur

WITH AN INTEREST IN JEWELLERY'S RELATION TO THE HUMAN BODY AND ITS INTERACTION WITH THE WEARER'S CLOTHES IT WAS ONLY A MATTER OF TIME BEFORE ART JEWELLER SONJA BISCHUR MADE THE MOVE TO FASHION. FROM BAGFRAME NECKLACES TO STRANDS OF PEARLS WHICH CAN BE BENT INTO ANY SHAPE, WHAT BISCHUR CALLS HER 'PURE JEWELLERY' REFLECTS THE DESIGNER'S PREOCCUPATION WITH FORM, FUNCTION AND TANGIBILITY.

Why did you change from art jewellery to fashion jewellery?
I got interested in fashion during the 90s when I saw designers like Issey Miyake and Comme des Garçons breaking the rules and pushing things further than anyone was doing in my own field. On the catwalk designers were being so radical – creating incredible, challenging pieces. Suddenly art jewellery felt rather narrow minded so in 2005 I made the switch to fashion jewellery.

What distinguishes the two fields?
To me, jewellery is an element of one's image therefore it belongs on the body and on clothing but art jewellery goes against that by being presented in a case.

With respect to my own work there's not much difference aesthetically but as an art jeweller I wasn't concerned with producing full collections – it was more about making one-off pieces. And art jewellery isn't subject to the same pressure of bi-annual schedules that fashion is, yet despite that, I feel freer working in a fashion arena.

What themes do you explore?
My initial inspiration tends to be a piece of fabric or an object whose shape I like. Then I become interested in its context and function. I like taking things that have had a previously defined function and re-contextualizing them. I'm also interested in where clothes end and jewellery

begins, so in most of my collections there is an interaction between textiles and more jewellery-based elements such as chains and beads.

How do these lines of inquiry translate into your work?
For the Bagframe necklaces (ss06) I used frames that had originally given form to purses and re-imagined them as necklaces so that they had no function other than to decorate. I like to use existing jewellery forms – such as engagement rings – and present them as something new. I made a pearl necklace but stiffened it with wire so that the wearer could mould it however they wished.

Another example is the collection of knitted tubes interwoven with wooden and glass bead necklaces that I made for aw07. One particular piece had a string of beads pulled through the arms of a sweater to create an item that could be a scarf embellished with a necklace or a necklace covered by scarf. There was no strict boundary and they couldn't be completely separated.

How has your art background influenced your fashion work?

I am interested in strong ideas and if I think something seems impossible I love the challenge of finding a solution. I like to explore with different materials and techniques so while each collection has similar themes the end result is very different.

Do you apply the same principles to your collaborative work?

Yes, although the thing about collaborating is that it often means working with someone else's ideas, which can be less easy to identify with. I made jewellery using feathers for an Austrian designer called Anne-Marie Herckes and in 1997 I was commissioned by Helmut Lang to make a tiara for his catwalk show. My dream job would be to work with Martin Margiela because I can relate to his ideas and way of approaching things.

Your work is quite minimal. What draws you to aesthetic simplicity?

Perhaps it's an Austrian thing – they say we like the simple life! I aim to work with materials in a way that is direct and elemental. I tend towards white, black and some grey because they're neutral and because I need to set some sort of boundaries I guess. That may change though – I recently started on a multi-coloured piece but if I were to evolve that idea the colours would have to be just right. Ultimately, I don't want to create difficulties for myself and I don't want my work to look 'built' so I try to find uncomplicated solutions.

For example?

The knotted fabrics in my ss07 collection. By repeatedly knotting fabrics such as poplin, chiffon or jersey and contrasting them with metal chains or beaded necklaces I was able to compose all sorts of structures. I kept the colours very monochrome: jet black, white and silver. The collection of necklaces culminated in a series of sculptural pieces made of shirts wound, knotted and draped around big beaded necklaces. My interest with those pieces, as with all my work, was the point at which I stop: where the piece is perfect but not overdone. It's reduced.

So, how do you know when that time has come?

When a piece has passed through my hands many, many times and I'm certain that it feels good.

PREVIOUS PAGE A KNOTTED RIBBON AND CHAIN FROM SONJA BISCHUR'S AW05 COLLECTION **OPPOSITE, LEFT** KNITTED TUBES THREADED WITH WOODEN BEADS BLUR THE BOUNDARY BETWEEN CLOTHES AND JEWELLERY IN BISCHUR'S AW07 COLLECTION **OPPOSITE, RIGHT** FOR SS07 KNOTTED SHIRTS ENTWINED WITH LARGE BEADED NECKLACES ALLOWED BISCHUR TO EXPLORE CONCEPTS OF STRUCTURE AND VOLUME **THIS PAGE, CLOCKWISE FROM BOTTOM LEFT** SHORTLY AFTER SWITCHING TO FASHION JEWELLERY FROM ART JEWELLERY SONJA BISCHUR WAS COMMISSIONED TO CREATE A COLLECTION OF TIARAS FOR HELMUT LANG'S AW97 CATWALK SHOW; KNOTTED FABRIC AND CHAIN NECKLACE AW05; SCARF AND CHAIN NECKLACE SS07; AS DEMONSTRATED BY THIS NECKLACE FROM HER SS07 COLLECTION A MINIMAL PALETTE INFORMS MUCH OF BISCHUR'S WORK

ABOVE AND ABOVE RIGHT A SCARF/NECKLACE HYBRID
FROM AW07 **OPPOSITE** A MODEL WEARS ONE OF SONJA
BISCHUR'S SS06 BAGFRAME NECKLACES

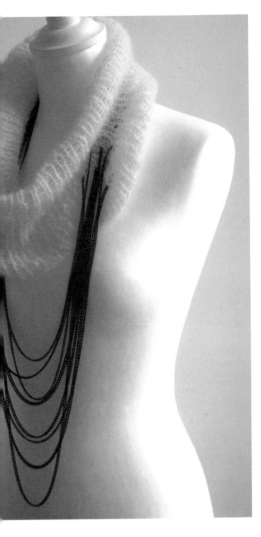

'I like to use existing jewellery forms – such as engagement rings – and present them as something new.'

Uli Raap

UNABLE TO FIND THE RIGHT MATERIALS WITH WHICH TO REALIZE HER NOVEL TAKE ON JEWELLERY ULI RAAP DECIDED SHE'D HAVE TO INVENT HER OWN. FUSING JERSEY AND RUBBER SHE CREATES SCREEN-PRINTED 'TEXTILE JEWELLERY' THAT COMBINES HISTORICAL DECORATIVE MOTIFS, AN OVER-THE-TOP SENSE OF SCALE AND A GENTLE DIG AT CONSUMER CULTURE.

When Uli Raap moved from her native Germany to Amsterdam in 1998 she was on a self-proclaimed mission to find a 'more daring approach to design.' Like all good quests Raap's voyage of discovery took a few turns (notably a degree in product design at Amsterdam's Rietveld Academy followed by an MA in applied arts) before she found her holy grail. These days, as a fully-fledged textile designer and artist, Raap applies her skills to a wide range of fabric-based projects and commissions, but it's for her jewellery that she has begun to establish a reputation within the fashion industry.

In order to create her debut collection Raap had to first develop a textile that would enable her to realize her vision. The result was, literally, a fusion of jersey with rubber which, once set, Raap screen printed with shimmering metal foil and rubber-based ink, then cut into elaborate necklaces, brooches and earrings. But although the collection referenced

the kind of regalia commonly depicted in sixteenth-century paintings (notably pearl chokers, Elizabethan neck ruffs and lace collars) the end results were more akin to a post-modern take on the trappings of a ghetto-fabulous life: giant diamonds, multi-stranded pearls and large-link chains printed up in neon colours and glittering metallic foils.

True to her art-based background Raap's work is her way of exploring very specific concepts and preoccupations. Her 'beauty with a twist' design philosophy is, she says, inspired by the female desire to be attractive and something to which she relates very strongly. 'I love beautiful objects and vibrant designs and I'm always searching through my work to find beauty (as relative as that might be) in new shapes, forms and colours.'

A less romantic source of inspiration, not to mention frustration, is the tyranny of consumer culture that engages her in an ongoing search to find new ways of

'...although the collection referenced the kind of regalia commonly depicted in sixteenth-century paintings... the end results were more akin to a post-modern take on the trappings of a ghetto-fabulous life.'

representing symbols of extreme affluence on textiles that are essentially worthless. Frustrated by what she sees as the herd mentality that underlies the 'safe choices' many of us make when buying jewellery or fashion accessories she produced items such as a range of brooches depicting designer It-bags and massive diamonds.

In general Raap says she prefers to work directly on the materials from the outset: 'The feeling I get just from touching the textiles is inspiring enough. Once I get my hands on the materials my ideas come very fast.' For particularly elaborate designs, however, she makes paper patterns to ensure a just-so fit. For now she makes everything in her own studio and she hopes to keep it that way so that she can stay in control of her production. She is, she says, very much a one-woman show and while she enjoys working on special commissions she has no immediate plans to become a large brand.

When asked who her jewellery appeals to she says that it is for anyone willing to embrace a little risk although, she insists, the beauty of her work is that it's actually very versatile: 'My jewellery can be worn with anything or even with nothing – I'll leave it to my customers to find the right combination. It's interesting to see how glamorous one of my chain-print necklaces can look on a little black dress and how casual it becomes when combined with a shirt and jeans.'

Although Raap sees herself as an artist she admits that she can understand why her jewellery has made an impact on the fashion scene. 'When my work was sold at L'Eclaireur in Paris I got a really positive reaction and it actually didn't surprise me that my jewellery works so well in a fashion context because it creates a strong image.' Furthermore, she says, she has thoroughly enjoyed the experience of discovering a new audience and would relish the opportunity to work with fashion designers in the future. For the time being she is extending her own repertoire with a range of screen-printed T-shirts emblazoned with the decorative prints from her jewellery.

Despite the early-days nature of her new direction Raap is already full of ideas for the future. 'Next I would like to create a very simple line that has two colours and very reduced shape – kind of a contrast to the overwhelming decoration I've been working with. My long term ambition, however, is to continue finding ways to surprise people with my work.'
WWW.ULI.NU

PREVIOUS PAGE IN THIS 'LOST IN LUXURY'
SHOOT A HARASSED DOG-LOVER PILES
ON THE PEARLS **THESE PAGES**
CLOCKWISE FROM BOTTOM LEFT BAG
BROOCH SS04; 'CHAINS' AND 'DIAMONDS'
NECKLACES FROM RAAP'S SS05
COLLECTION; 'PEARL' NECKLACE;
'MAIDENBLUSH' T-SHIRT EMBLAZONED
WITH A PRINTED PEARL NECKLACE AND
LACE PANEL AW03; THIS PORTRAIT OF
QUEEN ELIZABETH I INSPIRED THE
MAIDENBLUSH T-SHIRTS AS WELL AS
MUCH OF RAAP'S JEWELLERY AESTHETIC;
'FLOWER' NECKLACE

Wouters
& Hendrix

IN THE QUARTER CENTURY SINCE KATRIN WOUTERS AND KAREN HENDRIX FOUNDED THEIR COMPANY THEY HAVE LAUNCHED THREE SUCCESSFUL JEWELLERY LINES, PRODUCED MORE THAN 50 COLLECTIONS, AND OPENED TWO STAND-ALONE BOUTIQUES. AS INFLUENTIAL FIXTURES ON THE ANTWERP FASHION SCENE THEY HAVE ALSO CREATED BESPOKE JEWELLERY FOR A HOST OF TOP DESIGNERS, OR AS THEY PREFER TO CALL THEM, 'STAR QUALITY HOSTAGES'.

When asked 'what do you want to be when you grow up?' most kids harbour classic fantasies of the astronaut/cowboy/ air hostess variety. Katrin Wouters and Karen Hendrix were under no such illusions: 'We grew up during the new wave era which, creatively speaking, was a very liberated time. It was a period when every object could be an accessory – so from an early age we both had a thing about making jewellery.' In 1984, as fresh-faced graduates of Antwerp's Royal Academy of Fine Arts, the two friends put their goldsmithing qualifications to good use, produced their first joint collection and with it launched Wouters & Hendrix.

Skip forward to the present day and Wouters and Hendrix preside over an empire that includes two stand-alone boutiques – the flagship store which

opened in 2001 to sell their silver range, and a 'Gold Collection' showcase in 2007 from where they also sell their diamond jewellery. The secret of their success, says Hendrix, has been down to 'looking for new challenges so that designing never becomes a daily grind.' Pushing the limits, she adds, re-invigorates them.

Wouters and Hendrix produce much of their jewellery using ancient processes such as pliqué-a-jour – a process that involves making handmade gold and silver filigree frameworks into which coloured enamels are applied. Tracking down the few craftspeople and manufacturers who still carry out these techniques often requires considerable research and some foreign travel, but the detective work is always worth the effort. In addition to imbuing their work with a distinctive

flavour, Wouters believes that by using these old methods in novel ways: 'We are able to create our own unique story. Over time, jewellery acquires an emotional value and we hope our work resonates in the same way with our customers. We aim to produce something that is classic, humorous and obstinate.'

In 2004 Wouters & Hendrix celebrated 20 years in the business by launching a third line. My Favourites comprises pieces from the Gold and Silver collections, as well as one-off styles, which are now permanently for sale. 'We found it hard to come to terms with the fact that every six months we'd present a new collection and that our jewels only lasted for such a short time,' explains Hendrix of the thinking behind the venture. 'My Favourites means that we

PREVIOUS PAGE, LEFT THIS HAVANA CIGAR BOX FILLED WITH SEVEN WOUTERS & HENDRIX JEWELS WAS PRODUCED TO CELEBRATE THE LABELS' 20TH ANNIVERSARY **PREVIOUS PAGE, RIGHT** VINTAGE WOUTERS & HENDRIX EARRINGS **OPPOSITE** WOUTERS & HENDRIX'S GOLD COLLECTION WAS LAUNCHED IN 2007 AND THE 'MY FAVOURITES' COLLECTION WAS LAUNCHED IN 2004 TO CELEBRATE THE BRAND'S 20TH ANNIVERSARY. AS BOTH ARE PERMANENT COLLECTIONS THEY ARE NOT SUBJECT TO SEASONAL VARIATION. FROM LEFT: YELLOW GOLD-PLATED SILVER FILIGREE HOOP EARRINGS FROM 'MY FAVOURITES'; RING WITH SMOKY QUARTZ, BLACK ONYX DROP AND HAND-CARVED MOTHER-OF-PEARL FROM 'MY FAVOURITES'; A TRIPLE-BAND RING SET WITH SEMI-PRECIOUS STONES FROM THE 'SILVER' COLLECTION AW08 **THIS PAGE, CLOCKWISE FROM BOTTOM RIGHT** BRACELET FROM THE 'SILVER' COLLECTION AW09; NECKLACE FROM THE 'SILVER' COLLECTION AW09; LOOKBOOK IMAGE AND FINGERPRINT RING BOTH FROM THE 'GOLD' COLLECTION; NECKLACE FROM THE AW08 'SILVER' COLLECTION

'We aim to produce jewellery that is classic, humorous and obstinate.'

don't have to part with pieces that we feel are the strongest or to which we are most attached.'

When starting on a new collection Wouters and Hendrix favour working directly with the materials, the advantage of this approach being that they can try pieces out on the body, evaluate each other's creations and adjust the work accordingly. 'In this way, we end up with the different themes and models but because we work so closely together every piece is a creation by both of us.' As time goes on each new collection becomes part of an overall work-in-progress.

Another factor that keeps their interest piqued is collaborating with fashion designers. Over the years they have produced jewellery for the likes of Walter Van Beirendonck, Dirk Bikkembergs, Ann Demeulemeester, Dirk Van Saene, Paul Smith and Dries Van Noten. For the latter they designed jewellery for two of his catwalk collections (ss00 and aw06) which was later sold in Van Noten's stores. For the other designers they have at one time or another produced one-off pieces or provided Wouters & Hendrix own-line jewels for special events. 'Working with fashion designers is always a huge challenge but it enhances and enriches our own outlook and productivity,' says Wouters. 'We have to imagine ourselves immersed in their creative world and language, and then translate their themes and moods into a jewellery collection that corresponds with their style.'

Walks in the city and maintaining an open mind, says Hendrix, provide sufficient inspiration and although she claims neither she nor her partner actively follow trends they both acknowledge the indirect bearing they may have on their work: 'We all live in a media-saturated world and we all endure the same influences so unconsciously we are dealing with the same themes as designers everywhere. Perhaps it's inevitable they filter through somehow. But for us the word fashion doesn't have a negative connotation. Something fashionable does not mean that it cannot be timeless.'

WWW.WOUTERS-HENDRIX.COM

ABOVE SILVER BROOCH DESIGNED BY WOUTERS & HENDRIX FOR THE DRIES VAN NOTEN AW06 SHOW
OPPOSITE THREE PIECES FROM THE 'GOLD' COLLECTION. NOTE THAT EACH OF THE SEVEN RINGS SPORTS A DIFFERENT CHAIN MOTIF

Yazbukey

KOOKY, KITSCH AND PRETTILY PUNK ARE JUST SOME OF THE
ADJECTIVES USED TO DESCRIBE PARIS-BASED JEWELLERY AND
ACCESSORIES LABEL, YAZBUKEY. EQUAL PARTS PARISIAN CHIC
AND FLIRTY JOIE DE VIVRE YAZBUKEY JEWELLERY EMBODIES ITS
CREATORS' LOVE OF ALL THINGS FUN.

One evening in 2000 Yaz Kurhan found herself with an invitation to a party and a plain black dress in need of a makeover. Enlisting the help of her sister, Emel, she set to work with her sewing kit. A few snips, some beading and a couple of brooches later the newly-styled dress was the night's biggest hit and Yazbukey was born.

Today Yazbukey produce three distinct accessories lines: Precious, as the name suggests, is jewellery created from luxury materials such as gold, diamonds and precious stones. Signature pieces include the word Forever (and other romantic affirmations) cast in gold and wrought into enamel- and diamond-embellished bangles and chokers. Sur Mesure, launched in 2008 as the label's 'couture' collection, includes handmade brooches constructed from rhinestone-sprinkled rope curlicues and necklaces made from oxidized steel rings bound together with bright ribbons. Comprising an eclectic mix of materials that range from wood, leather and plastic to embroideries, fabrics and fur Sur Mesure has a craft-like, organic feel. But it is the main line of Swarovski crystal-studded Plexiglas jewellery for which Yazbukey are best known. Cartoonish, pop art-influenced motifs include cutesy animals, leg-flinging showgirls, old school telephones and the label's signature cocktail glass brooches.

With an exuberant more-is-more design philosophy Yazbukey is a 'playful universe' where inspiration is drawn from the things that make Yaz and Emel smile: Vincent Minnelli musicals, Gershwin's music, Grimm's fairytales and Tim Burton's films. Much as if they were stories or movies, each collection is given a tongue-in-cheek name: 'Either the rebel, the intellectual, or the playboy; which one is going to cover her with diamonds and gifts?'; 'Love me I'll be your nightmare' or 'I'm your Venus' – a series of articulated necklaces and brooches inspired by Hungarian porn star La Ciccolina.

As great-nieces of Egypt's King Farouk, Ottoman princesses Yaz and Emel have always led colourful lives. An itinerant childhood divided between Cairo and Istanbul furnished them with a unique view of the world. 'Travelling gives you a lot of memories that are not always a real vision,

PREVIOUS PAGE A TYPICALLY QUIRKY MONTAGE OF YAZBUKEY'S EXUBERANT JEWELLERY **THIS PAGE, CLOCKWISE FROM TOP LEFT** YAZBUKEY'S CREATORS OFTEN CALL ON FRIENDS TO MODEL THEIR WARES. HERE TWO GAME GIRLS SPORT THE 'HOTDOG' AND 'JACKIE-O' NECKLACES FROM THE SS09 COLLECTION; A MODEL POSES IN A PHOTO-BOOTH WEARING A TELEPHONE NECKLACE FROM THE MAINLINE SS08 COLLECTION (LEFT) AND A PIECE FROM THE 'SUR MESURE' SS08 COLLECTION (RIGHT); PERSPEX BUG BROOCH **OPPOSITE** CARTOON-LIKE JEWELLERY FROM THE SS08 MAINLINE COLLECTION

and our work is very influenced by that,' says Emel. When in Paris, where the Yazbukey studio is based, the girls can be seen at the coolest parties and often arrive accompanied by their pet chihuahuas Viktor and Kumpir. They are their own muses and they use themselves and their friends as canvases on which to project their vision.

Despite the whimsical nature of their work, however, the two sisters bring heavyweight industry experience to the table. Both graduated from the famed Studio Berçot in Paris, and before joining forces worked variously with Jeremy Scott, Martin Margiela, Givenchy and Christian Lacroix – for whom they created textile prints. But it was their industrial and graphic design studies undertaken before transferring to fashion that furnished them with the technical understanding that enables them to test materials' capabilities, create 3D-models and avoid the pitfalls inherent in creating jewellery.

When starting a new collection Yaz and Emel's approach is rigorous. They separate for up to a week, each to do their own research, after which they meet to bring the season's story to life. 'We try to merge both of our worlds together,' says Emel. Agreement is paramount – if one of them doesn't like an idea it is abandoned. Of working as a duo they say it turned them from sisters into friends. 'It's much better working with a sister because it's someone you can trust,' attests Yaz.

It's a winning formula that has seen Yazbukey go from strength to strength, garnering accolades and fans along the way. In 2003 they won the ANDAM (Association Nationale pour le Développement des Arts de la Mode) award for accessories from the French Ministry of Culture and their legion of high-profile devotees includes Björk, Gwen Stefani, Courtney Love, Mick Jagger and Kylie Minogue.

In addition to producing their own label they work as consultants on accessories ranging from shoes and bags to dogs' clothing and jewellery for clients including Christian Lacroix, Anna Molinari and Blumarine. During Paris fashion week their stuffed birds and wigs have appeared on the catwalks of Gilles Rosier and Gaspard Yurkievich respectively while a collection of Plexiglas necklaces for French designer Martine Sitbon led to their appointment as creative directors of the accessories collection for Sitbon's label Rue du Mail. For every project Yaz and Emel undertake their goal is simply 'to amaze'.

With boundless energy and humour the Yazbukey masterplan is to spread accessory love around the world. 'We want to establish a global chain of boutiques stocking our work. In particular we want to expand our jewellery collections as much as we can because to us jewellery is more important than clothes. Clothes date quickly but a beautiful jewel is timeless'.
WWW.YAZBUKEY.COM

Boasting an exuberant more-is-more design philosophy Yazbukey have created a 'playful universe' filled with things that make them smile.

Yoshiko
Creation Paris

IN THE SPIRIT OF HER HERO, THE FRENCH POET BAUDELAIRE, YOSHIKO KAJITANI BELIEVES
THAT 'THE BEAUTIFUL IS ALWAYS BIZARRE' AND THAT DESIGNING JEWELLERY IS AN ACT OF POETRY.
BIG ON METAPHOR AND LOADED WITH SYMBOLISM, YOSHIKO'S WORK IS PRESENTED IN QUIRKY
TABLEAUX, WHICH PAY HOMAGE TO THE DARKER SIDE OF HER FAVOURITE FAIRYTALES.

What does it say on your CV?
I studied fashion in Japan until I moved
to Paris in 1997 to take up fashion at
Studio Berçot. In Japan I learned how to
explore a concept and in Paris I learned
how to breathe life into a design. I also
gained some jewellery-making experience
at Erik Halley but for the most part
I'm pretty much self-taught: moulding,
sketching, even the taxidermy –
I worked it all out myself.

**When did you get your first
big break?**
I made a simple beaded necklace similar
to the ones African children wear and by
pure serendipity one day it caught the eye
of Sarah, the buyer from Colette. She liked
it and asked me to produce some pieces
for the boutique. That was my first
experience as a professional designer.

**With which fashion designers
have you collaborated?**
I collaborated with Yohji Yamamoto on
his Y's Red Label line for aw06. I was
inspired by tribalism and the idea of
clothes being like a second skin so I
embellished the garments with metal
parts to give them a slightly savage look.
When it came to working on the aw08
collection I created jewellery that was
inspired by the light of life coming out of
darkness. I also made a necklace that
looked like a big forest covered with
stuffed birds. One of the most exciting
things about that collaboration was that
Araki, of whom I am a huge fan,
photographed some of my pieces.

What did you learn from the experience?
Through working with one of Japan's
greatest fashion brands I also learned

a lot about creating an image and about
different ways of designing too.
For example, imagine a design that
incorporates a pearl: At Y's I would have
kept it very simple – not cutting, drilling
or processing it in any way. For my own
line I would treat the pearl so that
it became the focal point. In that way
I gained an awareness of the difference
in design philosophies.

What materials do you work with?
Mostly organic ones which I like to put
together with other things to create some
kind of conflict. For example: between
a stuffed animal and a piece of fake
fur; real leather and imitation leather;
or a natural stone and a piece of crystal.
I also make use of animal faces that are
normally thrown away or I recycle things
from the flea market.

PREVIOUS PAGE, LEFT THIS IMAGE FORMED THE FRONTISPIECE OF THE LOOKBOOK THAT ACCOMPANIED 'LE PETIT PRINCE – UNE MEMOIRE DE ROSE' – YOSHIKO CREATION PARIS' AW05 COLLECTION PREVIOUS PAGE, CENTRE AND RIGHT PORCELAIN DOLLS WERE USED TO CREATE BIZARRE TABLEUX FOR YOSHIKO'S SS06 COLLECTION 'ALICE'S ADVENTURES UNDERGROUND' OPPOSITE GOLD-PLATED ROSE BROOCH AND PENDANTS FROM AW06 THIS PAGE MAIN PICTURE SHOWS A COLLAGE OF PIECES FROM AW05; A SELECTION OF PIECES FROM AW06

'I'm pretty much self-taught: moulding, sketching, even the taxidermy – I worked it all out myself.'

THIS PAGE A MODEL WEARS A SELECTION OF JEWELLERY FROM 'LE FOSSILE' – YOSHIKO CREATION PARIS' SS07 COLLECTION **OPPOSITE** CLOSE-UP DETAILS OF THE ALL-WHITE, LACE-INSPIRED 'ALICE'S ADVENTURES UNDERGROUND' SS06 COLLECTION

What is your philosophy?
Design is not just about the outer layer – it can also affect our psychology at a profound level because our appearance and our state of mind are intimately connected to one another. So, I want my jewellery to make people feel beautiful but I also want it to break away from conventional jewellery. I want to choose more creative and original themes, so that everyone can interpret them in their own way.

What inspires you?
Alice in Wonderland, Irina Ionesco. Baroque decoration, The Little Prince, Beauty and the Beast, the tales of Lewis Carroll, museums, flea markets, a person's feelings and the earth. Life in Japan has different momentum from life in Paris.

For example, in Japan we're hugely affected by the seasons and we are really into technology. Paris, on the other hand, is about art and history.

In what ways does fashion influence your work?
Fashion influences my work and my life greatly. Nobody can be naked today and as I create I am always concerned with prevailing attitudes in fashion. It's very important to remember that fashion is a dream that motivates people.

What has been your greatest professional achievement?
The necklace I sold at Colette when I debuted. After that, opening my own store in Tokyo comes a close second.

Did you always want to create jewellery?
No. I was just hoping to get in an art school!

How do you keep your work original?
I give equal weight to subjectivity and objectivity.

How would you like to develop your brand?
When children see a dinosaur fossil they get really excited just by looking at it – that's how I want people to feel when they look at my jewellery. I don't want them to have to intellectualize it or even understand it. I want them to have that visceral, primitive response to my design. So, I guess what I'm saying is that I want Yoshiko Creation to be more like a natural history museum than an art gallery!
WWW.YOSHIKOCREATIONPARIS.COM

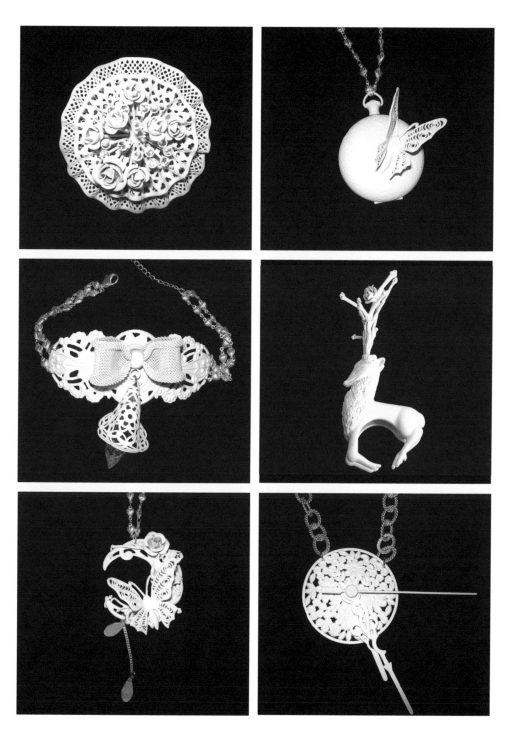

PICTURE CREDITS

LARA BOHINC
P.94 Photography left John-Paul Pietrus,
www.johnpaulpietrus.com
P.96 Photography left Linda Bujoli, Make-up
Tatyana Makaroya, Hair Cicci, Model Lucie Doublet
@ Nathalie Agency
All other photography Jernej Prelac

LAURA B
All Photography Andrea Vaggione

LIGIA DIAS
P.104 Photography Ligia Dias
P.106 Photography Ligia Dias
P.107 right Photography courtesy of Swarovski
PP.108 & 109 Photography Ligia Dias except
bottom right courtesy of Valery Demure
PP.110 & 111 All Photography Ligia Dias except
catwalk image www.firstview.com

MARION VIDAL
P.112 Photography Yann Robert
PP.114 & 115 Photography Marion Vidal
P.116 Photography top left and bottom Rebecca
Schweins Model Linde Stoel (Major Paris)
P.116 Photography top right Michael Wirth
www.michaelwirth.com
P.117 Photography Rebecca Schweins,
Model Linde Stoel (Major Paris)

MICHELLE JANK
P.118 Photography Harold David
(www.harolddavid.com)
P.120 Photography top right and left Harold David,
Hair/Make-up Claire Thompson
PP.120 & 121 Photography Still Lives
courtesy Valery Demure
P.122 Sketch left Michelle Jank
P.123 Photography top Jun Takahashi
PP.122 & 123 Photography still lives
courtesy Valery Demure

NAOMI FILMER
P.124 Photography Dan Lecca
P.126 All images courtesy Naomi Filmer
P.127 Photography left Naomi Filmer
P.127 Photography right courtesy Swarovski
P.128 Photography top left Dan Lecca
P.128 Photography bottom left Naomi Filmer
P.128 Photography right Dan Lecca
P.129 Photography all Gero Cacciatore
www.gerocacciatore.com

NATALIA BRILLI
P. 130 Photography Thomas Lillo
PP.132–135 All still life photography Julien
Classens and Thomas Deschamps
P. 134 Photography left Thomas Lillo
P. 135 Photography top right Luciana Val
and Franco Musso

PHILIP CRANGI
P.136 Photography left Dan Lecca
P.138 Photography left Steven Crawford
P.138 Photography right Dan Lecca
P.139 Sketch left Philip Crangi
P.139 Photography right Steven Crawford
P.140 Sketch Philip Crangi
P.141 Photography left Steven Crawford
P.141 Sketches all Philip Crangi

R
All Photography Gary Wallis

SABRINA DEHOFF
P.148 Sketch/Photography Sabrina Dehoff
PP.150 & 151 Photography Marcus Gaab
P.152 Photography Gene Glover
P.153 Photography top left & right
Daniel Josefsohn
P.153 Photography bottom both Alex Flach

SCOTT STEPHEN
P.154 & 155 Photography Kyoko Homma
Styling Remi Takenouchi Model Tasha
P.156 Photography top right Jonas Unger
Model Anna Korzun at Models 1
PP.156 & 157 All other images courtesy
Corinne Brun
P.157 All images courtesy Corinne Brun
PP.158 & 159 Photography all Corinne Brun

SCOTT WILSON
P.160 Photography Richard Bush,
Styling Sarah Richardson
P.162 Still life shots Antonio Marguet
www.antoniomarguet.com
P.162 Photography right Dan Lecca/
Matthew Williamson
P.163 Photography left firstview.com
P.163 Photography right catwalking.com
P.164 Photography top and middle Claire Robertson
P.164 Photography bottom Bruno Bazoud
P.165 Photography top left Antonio Marguet
www.antoniomarguet.com
P.165 Photography centre antheasimms.com
P.165 Photography top right Ram Shergill
P.165 Photography bottom right Bruno Bazoud

SHAOO
All images courtesy of WenWei Tong except
Bria Phillips
P.170 Photography right Bria Phillips

SONIA BOYAJIAN
P.172 Photography Sonia Boyajian
P.174 Photography & Sketches Sonia Boyajian
P.175 Photography Dan Lecca
PP.176 & 177 Photography & Sketches
Sonia Boyajian

SONJA BISCHUR
P.178 Photography Elfie Semotan,
Model Maria R, Styling Chris Pirnbacher
P.180 Photography Sonja Bischur
P.181 All images courtesy Sonja Bischur except
bottom left www.catwalking.com
P.182 Photography left David Auner Model Keila,
Styling Barbara Zach
P.182 Photography right Sonja Bischur
P.183 Photography Ola Bergengren Styling Karen
Langley Model Olya Ivanisevic

ULI RAAP
P.184 Photography left www.timmintiens.nl
PP.186 & 187 Photography all still lives Uli Raap
P.187 Photography top right Marijn de Jong
P.187 Photography bottom left Rinske Kreukniet
P.187 Photography bottom right © National
Museums Liverpool, Walker Art Gallery

WOUTERS & HENDRIX
PP.188 & 189 Photography Felix Tirry
P.190 Photography Rene Keller
P.191 Photography top left and middle Felix Tirry
P.191 Photography top and bottom right
Rene Keller

P.192 Photography Patrice Stable
P.193 Photography Rene Keller

YAZBUKEY
P.194 Photography Catherine Rouzies
P.196 Photography portraits taken in a photobooth
PP.196–199 all still lives courtesy Yazbukey

YOSHIKO CREATION PARIS
P.200 Photography Takao Oshima Styling Shun
P.201 Photography Takao Oshima Styling Shun
Art Direction Yoshiko Kajitani
P.202 Photography courtesy Yoshiko Creation
P.203 Photography Takao Oshima Styling Shun
P.204 Photography Takao Oshima Art direction
Yoshiko Kajitani
P.205 Photography courtesy Yoshiko Creation

ACKNOWLEDGEMENTS

Thank you to all the designers, photographers, PRs, stylists, models and bookers without whose time and talents this book would never have happened. Thanks also to all at Laurence King for backing this project, especially Helen Evans for her keen guidance and Sophie Page for her enthusiasm and encouragement. To everyone at & SMITH – thank you for bringing the book to life; to Christina Borsi – thanks for patience above and beyond the call. Cheers to Hywel Davies for always taking my calls; Corinne Brun for continuous support and Valery Demure for sharing her knowledge and contact book. For reasons too many to number thanks to Evie Gurney, Myles Quin, Claire Robertson, Gary Wallis, Donna Watson and Robb Young. And last but by no means least thanks always to my family: Ama, Aita and Kai.